Striving for Excellence in College

Striving for Excellence in College

Tips for Active Learning

SECOND EDITION

M. Neil Browne
Stuart M. Keeley

Bowling Green State University

Prentice Hall, Upper Saddle River, New Jersey 07458

Library of Congress Cataloging-in-Publication Data

Browne, M. Neil
  Striving for excellence in college : tips for active learning / M. Neil Browne, Stuart M. Keeley.—2nd ed.
    p. cm.
  ISBN 0-13-022058-2
    1. Study skills—United States.   2. Active learning—United States.   I. Keeley, Stuart, M., 1941–   II. Title.
  LB2395.B77   2001   99-048529

Editorial Director: Laura Pearson
Editor-in-Chief: Leah Jewell
Acquisition Editor: Craig Campanella
Editorial Assistant: Joan Polk
Managing Editor: Mary Rottino
Project Liaison: Fran Russello
Project Manager: Publications Development Company of Texas
Prepress and Manufacturing Buyer: Mary Ann Gloriande
Cover Art Director: Jayne Conte
Cover Designer: Bruce Kenselaar
Marketing Manager: Brandy Dawson

This book was set in 10.5/12 Berkeley Book by Publications Development Company of Texas and was printed and bound by Courier Companies, Inc.
The cover was printed by Phoenix Color Corp.

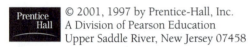 © 2001, 1997 by Prentice-Hall, Inc.
A Division of Pearson Education
Upper Saddle River, New Jersey 07458

Printed in the United States of America

10 9 8 7 6 5 4 3 2 1

ISBN 0-13-022058-2

Prentice-Hall International (UK) Limited, *London*
Prentice-Hall of Australia Pty. Limited, *Sydney*
Prentice-Hall Canada Inc., *Toronto*
Prentice-Hall Hispanoamericana, S.A., *Mexico*
Prentice-Hall of India Private Limited, *New Delhi*
Prentice-Hall of Japan, Inc., *Tokyo*
Pearson Education Asia Pte. Ltd., *Singapore*
Editora Prentice-Hall do Brasil, Ltda., *Rio de Janeiro*

CONTENTS

PART III: EXTERNAL CONDITIONS

PREFACE

We can all learn how to improve our mental performance. We wrote this book to help you become more like the learner you want to be—productive and engaged. Besides encouragement, what we have to offer are tips that skilled learners already know and use to their benefit. We want you to know them, too.

We have faith in your curiosity and desire for self-improvement. But you need specific guidance from experienced learners to move your natural inclinations along. Learning is a process that uses particular skills and attitudes to expand your awareness and appreciation. These skills and attitudes do not fall into place just because you go to school or get a little older. We all need teachers to give us the clues and strategies that will allow us to reach a point where we can feel confidence about our capability to learn on our own.

This book is a gift to you from two teachers who are your partners in learning. In fact, as we wrote the book, we found ourselves reminded of many tips that we needed to use more frequently as we, too, continue to learn. For example, we both get lazy at times just like any learner and forget to take careful notes when we hear a wonderful speaker, read a moving passage, or discover for the first time a creative scientific experiment. We included so many tips for learning that we guarantee you will find several that will jump-start your own learning. We hope this is a book that you will want to keep as a reminder of the many ways in which you can be a better learner tomorrow than you are today.

The aim of the book is not just learning, but *excellence* in learning. By excellence, we do not mean some lofty goal that only a few geniuses can hope to reach. Instead, we mean steady improvement toward *your* learning goals.

As you read this book, latch onto those tips that seem especially useful to you. The book is full of helpful hints, but you are the best judge of which ones will be beneficial as you continue to learn. We wrote the book so that college students, regardless of their current abilities, would finish the book with an expanded ability to think and learn more effectively, both during and after college.

This second edition has benefited from the constructive criticism of a number of students and teachers who used the first edition as a guide to excellence in college. In response to their suggestions and our own re-thinking, we have made the following changes in this new edition:

1. More examples of the active learning that *Striving* recommends.
2. Speed bump boxes that attempt to model how an active learner is always trying to think against the grain.
3. Active learning boxes that suggest how readers can practice what we are urging.
4. End-of-the-chapter web sites and supplemental reading.
5. Additional tips for active learning.
6. More emphasis on the joy of active learning.

With these changes and the help of our readers, old and new, we offer this celebration of the active learner.

M. NEIL BROWNE
STUART M. KEELEY

ACKNOWLEDGMENTS

We have the good fortune of knowing a large number of highly skilled learners. Many of them have helped us with this book. They provided actual models of thoughtful, active learners. Part of our task in writing the book has been trying to capture the strategies that we have seen them use so effectively as they sought excellence in college and then later in their careers.

We want to thank Carrie Williamson for her help with both the contents of the chapters and the graphics in the book. Several students and friends will notice their words somewhere in the text, so we should probably mention the generous help of Barb Keeley, Nancy Kubasek, Virginia Morrison, Andrea Giampetro-Meyer, and Mike Doherty. They seemed to enjoy recalling their own discovery of tips for active learning. We also wish to express our appreciation for the helpful comments of the following reviewers: Barbara Fowler, Longview Community College and Daryl Kinney, Los Angeles City College.

M.N.B.
S.M.K.

Striving for *Excellence* in *College*

MOUNTAINS MUST BE CLIMBED TO REACH THE OTHER SIDE

The quality of a person's life is in direct proportion to their commitment to excellence, regardless of their chosen field of endeavor.

—VINCE LOMBARDI

Close your eyes for a few minutes and let your imagination guide you. Try to join your distant historical cousins who were seeking a better life by traveling westward. They had heard stories of lush meadows, beautiful valleys, fertile farmland, as well as mines full of gold and silver. They weren't sure where they were going nor what would be there once they arrived, but full of hope, they started walking or riding toward a better life.

Tired and anxious, they would eventually see in the distance a frightening, awesome obstacle—the mountains. Face to face with a hurdle that seemed to mock them with its enormous bulk and treacherous terrain, they trudged ahead, determined and courageous. The easy thing to do would have been to turn back, but a surprisingly large number of them accepted the challenge presented by the mountains. We admire their drive and energy.

The title of this book contains a challenge for you. We have written it because we have faith that you want to be an excellent college student, not just an ordinary one. When we say excellent college student, we are not presenting you with a form of college life that is beyond your grasp. Nor do we believe that college is nothing more than assignments and books, as important as those both are. Rather, we have in mind a student, like you, who is preparing for a life of continual learning and who knows that the primary habits of mind required for such a life require an understanding of how to squeeze meaning from the confusing multitude of facts, ideas, and experiences. Central to this search for meaning are two fundamental skills: (1) the ability to think critically, to distinguish sense from relative nonsense and (2) the ability to think creatively, to generate new ideas and connections among ideas.

We began this book by talking about mountains because we are struck by the numerous similarities between the challenges presented by those huge structures and excellence in college. Let us show you:

Climbing Mountains	Striving for Excellence in College
As we hinted in our initial glance at mountains as an obstacle, they *can be* climbed.	Almost any college student with the right attitude and training can be an excellent learner.
Mountains are climbed, not all at once, but one rock or one hill at a time. Sometimes the going seems slow, but to reach the other side, you have to keep moving forward.	Excellence in college is achieved gradually. Many individual attitudes and skills must be developed, while attending class and studying. The goal is reached bit by bit, so patience is essential.
Climbing a mountain is made easier with a map and a human guide to help you conquer the adventures along the way.	Excellence in college is much more likely if you have some help. This book is your map; your professors and support services are the human guides, there to push you and encourage you to keep moving toward your goal of being a more complete learner.

Climbing Mountains	Striving for Excellence in College
The climb is more fun and probably more successful if you are joined by others who also want to get across the mountain.	Excellence in college is made more probable by your seeking that goal together with a network of supportive peers. While conquering educational challenges cannot be done for you, neither can it be done easily unless other students cooperate with your vision.
Climbing a mountain is tough work, work made rewarding only because there is absolutely no other way to get to the dream on the other side.	Striving for excellence in college is much more demanding than just surviving college. The drive for excellence is worth it because you want your mind to be better than it was when you came to college. You have seen people who clearly have developed their mental capabilities and are using them with great skill. To imitate them, you must overcome obstacles that stand in your way on a college campus.
Actually getting over the mountain may not be any more important than the fact that the climbers were willing to struggle against the avalanches, slippery ledges, and fatigue that stood in their way.	Striving for excellence in a college is a wonderful compliment to your character. Of course, you should try to reach your goal of excellence, but you deserve enthusiastic praise for being willing to make the necessary effort to pursue the goal at all.
Climbing the mountain takes you to crisper air, open spaces, and clear skies. Stopping on the way over the mountain surely is better than never having started the climb.	The road to excellence in college consists of many steps. Taking some of the steps is better than taking none. Excellence is a matter of degree. Your goal should be to improve your capability as a learner. By taking any of the many steps in this book, you will be closer to your goal.

Notice how important it is to acquire knowledge and information as you climb mountains and learn how to learn more effectively. We need to study maps as we climb mountains; we need to learn important information and ideas as we strive toward excellence in college.

ACTIVE LEARNING AND EXCELLENCE IN COLLEGE

This comparison between climbing mountains and striving for excellence in college has one powerful similarity that deserves special emphasis:

Neither can be achieved simply by watching others. You must be a full, ACTIVE participant to get the job done.

Watching someone else dance, sing, or learn is relatively easy. We can even fool ourselves into thinking that simply being an observer is a productive approach to achievement. The temptation to just watch is powerful.

But the passive approach to college is one of the most destructive strategies you could choose. It actually reduces your possibilities; it makes you into a sponge. Sponges absorb the liquids they encounter. After they absorb, they are prepared only to release the same liquid they have absorbed.

When learners permit themselves to play the role of sponge, they prepare themselves to be a sponge and nothing more! They can repeat what they heard, period. They are carrying someone else's message. Their creativity and mental development have either been repressed or sharply limited.

This book contains tips for you. Our belief is that you can play the major role in improving your mind; you don't have to wait on others to tell

SPEED BUMP 1-1

But isn't it a lot of hard work to be excellent?
And who will notice anyway?

Think back to the last time that you accomplished a goal. Did you win a basketball game or ace a difficult exam? Remember the feeling—the excitement, the relief, the confidence that you could probably do it again! Learning and applying the tips in this book will give you a similar sense of excitement. You will be a better student, person, and citizen with each learning obstacle you overcome. However, you may not be patted on the back by professors in college or your boss at work. When you think no one appreciates all of your hard work, remember that some of the most rewarding events in your life have been those you have worked long and hard to achieve, even though no one may have persuaded or bribed you to do them. Excellence of any kind requires hard work; it is special because it is not easy. Yet, in the end, there is usually some kind of payoff, whether it comes in the form of a pay raise, scholarship, or public recognition. Achieving excellence in college will make you a more educated, knowledgeable, and persuasive human being. And, perhaps that is the best reward of all!

zena

zena

you what to think and how to organize it. By trying our tips, even a few of them, you should get a sense of the personal strength that comes from guiding your own learning.

Framing College as a Beginning Rather Than an End

Attending college has multiple benefits. You already know that being in college is a step toward a career, a most important step. But striving for excellence in college is based on the recognition that your life consists of a career plus much, much more. Sometimes you will be alone, just you and your mind. Many of your most enjoyable times will be spent with family and friends. Finally, you are a neighbor and citizen. In these latter roles, the rest of us are depending on you. We need your careful reasoning to help us; we need the fruits of your excellence in college.

In each of these roles, your mind will work only as well as it has been trained. Your professors and books are all pledged to help you function more effectively in any role you choose in life. You can probably survive or just get by with the mental attitudes and skills you currently possess. But we believe you want to go to a higher level.

As professors ourselves, we want to encourage you to develop the ability to go beyond what we have to teach you. In simple terms, we want to help you become active learners so that you can use college like a trampoline to propel you far beyond where you will be when you graduate. If we can play that role, we will have helped you see college as a beginning, not the end of your learning.

Striving for Excellence in College: Its Organization and Logic

The plan of this book should make sense to you. Each of the three parts is fundamental to your excellence as a learner. The first focuses on attitudes. This section is first because just as no mountain gets climbed unless certain attitudes are present, active learning is impossible unless specific attitudes are present. An important message in the section about learning attitudes is the role played by you in shaping these attitudes.

The second section builds on the first by focusing on knowledge about how to learn more effectively. We are struck by the emptiness of advice to students to "study harder" or "plan more effectively" unless that advice is followed by step-by-step suggestions about what to do to reach the goal. This book gives you dozens of specific things you can do to help your learning.

The third section recognizes that the mixture of attitudes and skills that you bring to and develop in college are put to use in a particular environment. Your college, peers, and professors provide the context that promotes or limits your active learning. This third and final section suggests how you can maximize the positive aspects of this environment.

Within the sections, each chapter after Chapter 1 shares a common framework. The first step is a self-assessment that serves as an orientation to the subject matter of the individual chapter. Completing those self-assessments lets you know where you are at the start in terms of the advice contained in the chapter.

Next the need for the chapter is revealed in the form of an obstacle you must overcome. As we told you, excellence in college is no easy task. It is doable, but requires your best. Each obstacle is a potential problem standing in your way, threatening your mental progress. By naming and describing it, we are taking the initial step that will permit us to leap over it.

The third part of each chapter is the meat. Here is where we explain the tips that only the best students know and use to overcome the obstacles. We intentionally gave you many tips so you could pick and choose the ones that *you* think will work for you. Following *some* of the tips is better than ignoring all of them.

The Quick Review Box at the end of each chapter contains a convenient list of the tips for active learning discussed in that chapter.

Mountains have been crossed, and you can achieve excellence in college. Study the tips and discuss them with your teacher and peers. Like any other activity, it is more doable with the help of others.

Part I
Attitudes

TAKING CHARGE OF YOUR OWN LEARNING

People often say that this or that person has not yet found himself. But the self is not something one finds; it is something one creates.

—THOMAS SZASZ

We know what we are, but know not what we may be.

—SHAKESPEARE

SELF–ASSESSMENT

You are just starting your second week in a college course. You were really overwhelmed the first week. First, the professor called on you to answer really hard questions. You did not answer any of the questions very well. Second, the professor assigned long, difficult articles that were hard for you to understand. Finally, the other students did not seem to be having problems. Do you:

a. Drop the class because you are not a good enough student to be in this class?

b. Grumble about how hard the professor is making the class?

c. Accept the probability that you will get a low grade?

d. See the course as a personal challenge, and schedule a meeting with the professor?

OBSTACLES

■ Lack of self-confidence

■ Self-defeating beliefs

■ Fear of failure

■ Blaming factors beyond our control

■ Lack of curiosity

Let us begin this chapter by sharing an important equation with you:

Strong Attitudes + Good Strategies = Excellence in College

Striving for excellence as a learner requires certain attitudes on your part. Many people with great natural ability have failed to "be all they could be"; many without natural ability have achieved excellence. For example, athletes who have achieved excellence may or may not have had exceptional natural abilities; but all of them have held certain attitudes. People like Michael Jordan possess attitudes that move them beyond the ordinary. Sure, they face obstacles, but the attitudes highlighted in this chapter help change the obstacles into opportunities.

Attitudes are interesting. Some promote our personal growth. Others hold us back. An essential positive attitude for excellence in college is a "take charge" attitude—the belief that your education is under your personal control and that you can and will take whatever steps are necessary to achieve the goals that you set for yourself. Below, we describe a number of negative attitudes that present obstacles to your taking charge of your learning. Then we provide tips for overcoming them.

Lack of Self-Confidence

Seeing ourselves as inadequate, incompetent, worthless, stupid, or lazy keeps us from striving for excellence. Such attitudes make us feel that we don't deserve success in college or that we don't, and never will, have the ability to achieve it. These self-defeating self-images have many sources, including parental and teacher messages, unsuccessful learning experiences, and negative thinking habits that we have developed.

Self-Defeating Beliefs

Almost all of us have allowed ourselves at times to believe a huge assortment of things that keep us from achieving what we could achieve. But just imagine how tough it is to achieve excellence in college if you tell yourself any of the following:

- I should be perfect in all possible respects.
- I must be applauded or loved by virtually every person that I might encounter.
- I would die if I ever did anything stupid.

As you can well imagine, such beliefs make it difficult for us to take on challenges, to try something new, to push ourselves beyond our "comfort zones." For example, if you were to believe that you should be thoroughly excellent in everything you do, you would avoid asking questions in class, because you might ask a question that others would see as stupid. Successful learners try to recognize these destructive beliefs and resist them with more productive beliefs—the kind that will move you toward excellence.

Fear of Failure

Another attitudinal obstacle to taking charge of our learning is a need to "play it safe," to stick with what we are already comfortable with, to avoid taking risks. If we fear making mistakes, we are not likely to try new learning strategies, to put ourselves into situations in which we might fail. For example, if we know we can succeed within the sponge model of learning, why risk active learning?

This attitude is similar to that of a tennis player with a very successful serve who chooses to keep practicing the serve instead of working on an area of her tennis game that is very weak; she never will reach the excellence as a tennis player that she seeks. Playing it safe is comfortable, but it does not encourage us to grow.

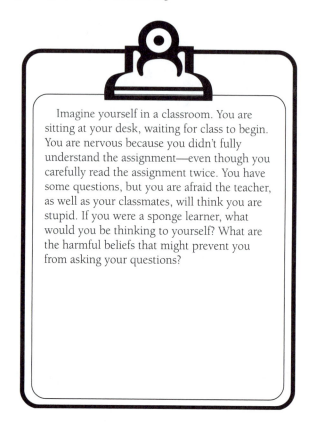

Imagine yourself in a classroom. You are sitting at your desk, waiting for class to begin. You are nervous because you didn't fully understand the assignment—even though you carefully read the assignment twice. You have some questions, but you are afraid the teacher, as well as your classmates, will think you are stupid. If you were a sponge learner, what would you be thinking to yourself? What are the harmful beliefs that might prevent you from asking your questions?

Blaming Factors Beyond Our Control

Think for a minute. Why do you think most things happen to you? Luck? Your environment? Other people? Or your own decisions? Too many of us blame everything but ourselves for what happens to us. It is convenient to see our life as shaped by others, rather than accepting some responsibility for how it develops. For example, we might see our success in college as at the mercy of our teachers or our parents. This attitude prevents us from taking charge of our own lives.

■ Lack of Curiosity

Striving for excellence in college requires active curiosity—a strong desire to know what is going on around us, to understand things, to make connections. We are not likely to take charge of our learning if we do not form the habit of looking for opportunities to learn as well as looking for new ways to learn. Successful learners are curious about the world.

SPEED B^U^{M}P 2-1

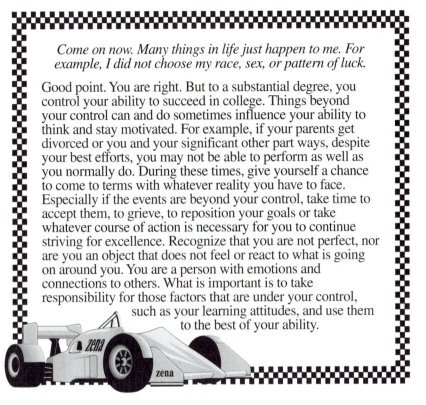

Come on now. Many things in life just happen to me. For example, I did not choose my race, sex, or pattern of luck.

Good point. You are right. But to a substantial degree, you control your ability to succeed in college. Things beyond your control can and do sometimes influence your ability to think and stay motivated. For example, if your parents get divorced or you and your significant other part ways, despite your best efforts, you may not be able to perform as well as you normally do. During these times, give yourself a chance to come to terms with whatever reality you have to face. Especially if the events are beyond your control, take time to accept them, to grieve, to reposition your goals or take whatever course of action is necessary for you to continue striving for excellence. Recognize that you are not perfect, nor are you an object that does not feel or react to what is going on around you. You are a person with emotions and connections to others. What is important is to take responsibility for those factors that are under your control, such as your learning attitudes, and use them to the best of your ability.

TIPS ONLY THE BEST STUDENTS KNOW

> **TIP 1** Think about your self-image as central to your learning and as always evolving.

The bad news is that certain self-images prevent us from successfully striving for excellence; the good news is that your self-image is changeable and under your control. You are responsible for how you perceive yourself. None of us is either all good or all bad, totally worthwhile or totally worthless—even though sometimes we may think that way.

Instead, we have certain strengths and weaknesses, certain interests and values, and certain feelings and reactions—and all of these are changeable—at least to some extent. All of us have the capacity to define who we are and to make value judgments about which characteristics we like and don't like.

Thus, your self-image isn't something permanent, something you are stuck with. You can change it.

Students pursuing excellence need self-images that encourage active learning. Let's check your self-image at this time. How do you view yourself as a learner? Make a list of learning characteristics that apply to you. Now, compare your list to a list that we have made of characteristics that apply to "take charge" active learners:

Self-image of active learners

- Curious
- Eager for challenges
- Feeling responsible for their learning
- Desiring to improve their learning potential
- Looking forward to finding new information
- Confident that they can learn

Although those striving for excellence will not all have the same self-image, they will be very similar. These self-images act as a gyroscope, or an internal guide, for the active learning process, and are crucial to becoming an active learner. Perhaps a number of these do not yet comfortably fit your self-image. We encourage you to consider their potential benefit, to recognize that your self-image is not carved in stone.

▶ **TIP 2 Accept personal responsibility for your learning.**

Striving for excellence means taking personal responsibility for your own education, recognizing that what and how you learn is not up to your teachers; it is *up to you.* This attitude requires that you look inside yourself as the most important source of your learning.

Taking personal responsibility means demanding more of yourself, overcoming the fears and anxieties associated with increased self-reliance, planning your own learning strategies, and not making excuses and placing the blame on others when you do not succeed. It means recognizing that teachers are not responsible for your learning; you are. It means recognizing that you are not at the mercy of educational annoyances like boring teachers, silly assignments, poorly designed exams, inconveniently placed libraries and books, and enjoyable distractions.

▶ **TIP 3 Focus on the process of learning, not just the results.**

Avoid believing that it is an absolute necessity for you to succeed perfectly to be a worthwhile person. Instead, you should strive toward becoming *your* best as a learner, rather than *the* best. Remember: There will always be people who achieve more than you, and that's okay. You are just trying to achieve as much as *you* can.

Focus on enjoying the *process* of striving for excellence, rather than the end results, such as grades, parental approval, and honors. Learning is incredible fun if we just open ourselves to its rewards. Strive for your own sake, rather than to please others.

▶   **TIP 4   Take risks to build self-confidence.**

You will not take steps to strive for excellence as long as you believe you can't succeed! Lack of confidence is a major obstacle. Fortunately, like your self-image, self-confidence is not a fixed entity. But, how do we develop self-confidence?

People who lack confidence underestimate what they are capable of doing. They are saying to themselves, "I don't think I can," as well as, "And if I can't, that would be awful." This attitude keeps them from trying activities that seem hard or risky. Yet, self-confidence comes from mastering difficult activities.

We need to see ourselves as potentially competent to feel self-confident, and we need to feel confident to try activities that allow us to feel competent. One way to break out of this vice is to force yourself to try activities in class and strategies for completing assignments that are new to you. Then prepare much better than ordinary for those new experiences.

By following this strategy, you will have increased your chances for performing in an excellent fashion. The more activities you try, the more alternative pathways to learning that you are likely to master; from that experience, more and more self-confidence is created. Then the next time you encounter difficult assignments or classroom projects, you will be quick to give them a try.

▶   **TIP 5   Tolerate your mistakes.**

Striving for excellence takes you out of your sponge model "comfort zone." It requires you to try new things, to change who you are as a learner; it forces you into uncharted waters. It presents you with both the excitement and the fears of meeting a challenge. The trick is to overcome the fears.

The most important cause of fears associated with risk is the set of rather automatic self-defeating thoughts that we associate with the possibility of failure. Such thoughts include:

"This is just too hard."

"It would be horrible if I fail."

"I might make a mistake, and that would be awful."

"I might look stupid; and if I do, that would be horrible."

"My teacher will make fun of me if I ask a bad question."

You need to fight such thoughts by welcoming your mistakes and errors, rather than being afraid of them, and using them as helpful feedback. Accept the need to practice, practice, and practice again those things you find most difficult—the things you are most likely to make mistakes at. Accept the fact that human beings—like yourself—are limited and regularly make mistakes—and that's okay.

➤ **TIP 6   Don't let unrealistic shoulds stand in the way of your excellence.**

Extreme, self-demanding, and unforgiving beliefs like the following prevent us from taking charge of our learning:

- I should be completely excellent.
- I should never make mistakes.
- I should be able to find a quick solution to every problem.

Self-Defeating Image

Active Learner's Self-Image

Some shoulds are helpful in guiding our lives, but others have no basis in reality and are self-defeating in nature. For example, if you have the belief that you should always be excellent at every thing you try, you are bound to fail, and to be at the mercy of your own harsh and unfair self-assessment. After all if you have this belief and are not excellent in some activity, then the logical conclusion is that you are a pretty worthless human being.

The solution? Discover, challenge, and revise your shoulds. When you have feelings that are keeping you from taking charge of your learning, look for the shoulds! You will probably find some. Then check them out. Are they true? Are they exaggerations? Where did they come from? Is that a good source? Are they self-defeating?

When you have concluded that shoulds are defeating your self-esteem, you need to combat them with beliefs that make more sense, are more accurate, and are more self-enhancing. In fighting shoulds, it is helpful to remember that in most situations, replacing shoulds with "It would be preferable" or "It would be nice" will give you a more realistic view of the situation and lead to actions that are more self-enhancing, such as active problem solving. Examples of how you can work to change your self-defeating shoulds include:

1. Event: Getting ready to ask questions in class

   Should belief: I should always be perfect and not make mistakes.

   Effect on behavior: Anxiety, avoidance of asking questions

   Anti-should belief: That belief is too absolute. I'm just learning. It would be nice if I could be perfect while learning, but that's not possible, because I am just a human being. The more mistakes I am willing to make, the more I can learn.

2. Event: You can't find something in the library that you need for a paper.

   Should belief: If I need something, I should be able to get it without hassle.

   Effect on behavior: Frustration, giving up

   Anti-should belief: Who gave me this rule? Where is the evidence for it? It would be nice if there were always an easy solution to problems, but I don't rule the world. What can I do about this inconvenient situation?

   Effect on behavior: Doing something constructive to work on the paper

When we change our beliefs, we also change both our feelings and our ability to act.

QUICK REVIEW BOX

1. Think about your self-image as central to your learning and as always evolving.

2. Accept personal responsibility for your learning.

3. Focus on the process of learning, not just the results.

4. Take risks to build self-confidence.

5. Tolerate your mistakes.

6. Don't let unrealistic "shoulds" stand in the way of your excellence.

PLACES TO SEARCH FOR MORE ON THIS TOPIC

Albert Ellis and R.A. Harper, *A New Guide to Rational Living* (Wilshire Books, 1997).

"Techniques for Disputing Irrational Beliefs (DIBS)," *The Albert Ellis Reader,* ed. by Albert Ellis and Shawn Blau (Citadel Press, 1988).

Martha Davis, et al., *The Relaxation and Stress Reduction Workbook* (New Harbinger, 1995). Especially beneficial are the chapters on "Goal Setting and Management," "Refuting Irrational Ideas," and "When It Doesn't Come Easy."

CHAPTER 3

RESISTING THE NEED TO BE ENTERTAINED

The happiness that is genuinely satisfying is accompanied by the fullest exercise of our faculties and the fullest realization of the world in which we live.

—BERTRAND RUSSELL

SELF-ASSESSMENT

You are trying to schedule your classes for the next semester. You had a really heavy load this semester, and you think you might be ready for a break. In just one of your classes, you had to write eight papers and read twenty-page reading assignments for each class. The professor expected you to talk a lot in class, so you had to be really prepared. You met with the professor several times outside of class, and you decided that you liked her even though she was somewhat intimidating. But, she was just not very exciting. Do you:

  a. Schedule your classes based on your need for sleep.
  b. Schedule several easy classes that your roommate took this last semester.
  c. Think about taking the same professor again, but decide that your schedule will be hard enough without her course.
  d. Schedule the challenging professor you had last semester. Your hard work in that course paid off; you learned a lot.

OBSTACLES

■   The great attractiveness of being entertained

■   Low frustration tolerance

■   Focusing on immediate, rather than long run, results

Achieving excellence as learners requires that we learn to overcome some of our natural tendencies. We are inclined to prefer pleasure to pain, comfort to discomfort, being entertained to working hard, and immediate pleasure to delayed pleasure.

Yet, think back to the times that you have had the most meaningful learning experiences: Perhaps when you learned to play the piano, or learned a foreign language, or excelled at a sport, or solved a difficult problem. Or imagine what it must have been like for Olympic athletes to achieve excellence in their chosen sports or for scientists to develop vaccines for diseases. We all realize that in each of these cases, much discomfort must be endured, much immediate pleasure has to be sacrificed, and much frustration has to be tolerated. Achieving excellence is difficult, often frustrating work.

Now, imagine times when you have been in a passive entertainment mode: Perhaps a trip to Disney World, watching a movie or a television sitcom, listening to a comedian, or hearing a dynamic lecturer who tells amusing stories. Such experiences provide much immediate fun and pleasure, but do they promote excellence in learning? Not very often!

Our minds are too passive during such experiences. They are not in an active, reflective mode. Giving in to our needs to be entertained, we risk the possibility of the warning communicated in the title of a book by social critic Neil Postman, *Amusing Ourselves to Death.* A weekend in a major city or at a lake can be a great get-away vacation; but when we seek entertaining experiences in our education, we run the danger of becoming contented robots rather than critical and creative thinkers.

SPEED B$^{U M}$P 3-1

But I love to be entertained. Why are you so opposed to entertainment?

We're glad you asked. We thought to ourselves that what we were saying was just a bit more stuffy than what we had intended.

Let us be clear. We love to be entertained, just as you do. But what we are emphasizing is the need to keep learning goals in mind. If entertainment is assisting your understanding and your critical thinking skills, by all means, seek out that entertainment. But so often entertainment is just that. It is enjoyable, period. Active learning provides a deeper pleasure, one linked to personal growth and awareness. But the road to that more permanent happiness is not always fun-filled. That message is what we are trying to share.

An obstacle highly related to the need to be entertained is the obstacle of low frustration tolerance (LFT). As learners, we display LFT when we are unable to withstand the discomfort of a particular learning situation, such as a homework assignment, and believe that we *MUST NOT BE UNCOMFORT-ABLE*. Statements like, "This is too hard; I can't stand it," " I shouldn't have to do this because I don't like it," and "I can't get this; I give up" all indicate LFT.

What is responsible for LFT is the belief that we should be comfortable and free from pain at all times. Life should always be comfortable.

When we are prone to LFT, we have difficulty sticking with learning tasks that are demanding and challenging, or choosing professors who challenge our minds and make us work hard. We prefer tasks that have immediate solutions or provide immediate pleasure and prefer professors who do the thinking part for us.

We rarely make gains without initially experiencing some discomfort, and the so-called easy way usually does not help you reach the long-term goal of excellence. If we are going to walk up a mountain stream to bathe in a waterfall, we're probably going to have to step on stones and rocks to get there. Long-term gains initially demand short-term discomfort. However, *with practice,* you will look forward to the rewards of overcoming challenging learning situations and the discomfort that goes with them, much as we all enjoy solving a complex puzzle.

An obstacle closely related to LFT is our habit of focusing on immediate rewards, rather than delayed rewards. The problem with this tendency is that seeking immediate gains almost always costs us in the long run. Eating lots of cake and pie gives us abundant short-term pleasure but keeps us from getting in shape for spring break. Similarly, passively listening to entertaining lectures that lack much substance may provide us with much short-term intellectual pleasure but divert us from developing our own thinking processes—something that takes much long-term effort.

Fortunately those of us striving for excellence can, if we pay attention, learn to tolerate discomfort and frustration.

Tips Only the Best Students Know

▶ **TIP 1   Focus on the long-run benefits of active learning.**

When approaching learning tasks, ask yourself, "What do I want in the *long run?* What are my long-term goals as a learner? Do I want to retain what I learn for lengthy periods of time? Do I want to actively decide what to believe? Do I want to be in charge of my learning?"

Just as is true for LFT, the need to be entertained supports short-run learning. As learners, we are like persons looking for an easy way to keep in physical shape. We want gain without pain.

When you are engaged in a difficult learning task, ask yourself, what can I do that will be most helpful to me in the long run? Do I need to be actively taking notes? Should I be asking questions? When choosing professors, ask yourself how you can choose in such a way as to maximize learning. Perhaps the challenging, frustrating, "hard" professor may cause discomfort in the short run, but provide the basis for major gains in the long run.

▶ **TIP 2   Start small and take small steps.**

In striving to climb high mountains, it is very scary to stand at the base and eye its summit. What a long way to climb! But learning to climb mountains becomes much more doable when we think of the task in terms of a series of small steps, each of which can be accomplished—such as moving progressively in small steps to each subsequent plateau, peak, or ridge.

You can apply this same strategy to learning to handle any frustration and stress that you feel while striving for excellence in college.

How can you use this small-step strategy to tolerate frustration and overcome the need to be entertained? One way is to *plan ahead*. Define your long-term goal in specific terms, then define small subgoals that are steps for reaching that goal. Goals might include, for example, persisting with a difficult homework assignment for three straight hours, or writing down five critical thinking questions following a lecture.

Then ask, How close to the goal am I and what goals would represent small improvements? If you usually give up on a difficult task after 30 minutes, you might set an improvement subgoal of 45 minutes of concentrated effort.

Remember: Rome wasn't built in a day, all the great books can't be read on a weekend, and you can't lose 20 pounds for that spring break trip in a week. Accomplishing important personal goals takes planning, time, and remembering the need for taking small steps at a time.

▶ **TIP 3   Reward yourself for small improvements and overcoming LFT.**

Sometimes learning is its own reward. But sometimes we need help getting started because rewards for behaviors that compete with active learning tend to be powerful. In addition, many rewards for active learning are quite delayed. Thus, it makes sense to find ways to reward ourselves. When we self-reward, we take charge of our own learning and make it harder for ourselves to give in to the powerful and immediate rewards we get from behaviors that compete with learning, such as socializing, drinking, sleeping and eating.

What you want to do as a self-rewarder is gradually demand more from yourself. Break the learning task down into small, workable steps, each getting you closer to your goal, and reward yourself for achieving the small steps. Rewards should be something that you find personally desirable, such as food, a CD, or a special activity. Then gradually make the steps larger in subsequent learning tasks until you get to a point where your motivational level is high enough that you don't need to self-reward.

▶ **TIP 4   Challenge thoughts that promote LFT.**

Certain automatic ways of thinking tend to accompany LFT. One way to move toward high frustration tolerance (HFT) is to aggressively challenge such thoughts. First, let's examine some beliefs that promote LFT. When you are feeling frustrated with some learning task, such as a difficult homework reading assignment, see whether you might be thinking some of the following:

"This is too difficult; I shouldn't have to work so hard."
"What a hassle (. . . and why should I have to be hassled?)!"
"Studying should be painless."
"I should be able to get this with little effort; it's awful that I can't."

The next step is to work on challenging these thoughts and replacing them with thoughts consistent with HFT:

- Where's the evidence (that I can't stand it, that things should be easier)?
- What is the proof (that I can't stand it, etc.)?
- Why must things be different than they are?
- How would that be so terrible?
- Can I survive even if I don't get what I want right away?
- How bad would it be if I had to put up with discomfort for awhile?
- What are the benefits of tolerating frustration for a longer period of time?

The answers to these questions serve as powerful hints for how you can fight LFT. Here are some ways "to talk to yourself" to promote HFT:

"There is no evidence that I can't stand it; I can tolerate discomfort even though I may not like it."
"There is no reason that there should be gain without pain; in fact, the evidence suggests the opposite."
"The long term benefits really do outweigh the short term discomforts."
"It's inconvenient that things are not the way I'd like them to be, and it would be desirable to do the best I can under the circumstances; if I can't 'get it' right away, it's not awful."
"I don't like it, but I can stand it."

As you practice new ways of thinking, you can start to see frustrations as a regular and necessary part of achieving excellence, and you can tell yourself, "If I haven't had at least half a dozen frustrations in a day, then I just may be amusing myself to death."

TIP 5   Practice "standing it."

Fortunately, frustration and discomfort won't kill us. We are not fragile. You can increase your ability to tolerate frustration and discomfort by practicing tasks you previously defined as unbearable or too much of a hassle. Be like a bicyclist who relishes the chance to charge up a steep hill—rather than the one who goes around the hill to avoid the challenge.

For example, if you have a professor who frustrates you by his persistent questioning, raise your hand in class more often to get practice standing the frustration. To get even more practice, actively seek out challenging professors, ones who make you think and refuse to provide you with immediate answers to questions. Or if you find particular kinds of reading assignments especially frustrating because you can't immediately understand them, sit down with such assignments and practice "staying with it" for increasing lengths of time.

TIP 6   Surround yourself with others who have HFT.

It is much easier to tolerate high frustration and stress levels when others around us are also doing so. We feel a sense of community and support and much less group pressure to value entertainment over hard work.

One way to meet HFT people is to seek out challenging classes with challenging professors. Also, look for people in any of your classes who seem to be well prepared and tend not to procrastinate. Procrastination is one of the clearest signs of LFT.

TIP 7   Break difficult learning activities into small parts.

Sometimes, regardless of how hard you work, a task in college is too tough for your present skill level. For example, you encounter the writings of some philosopher who writes with such complexity that you can't understand her without other background information. Or instructors assign reading materials to you that assume background knowledge that you don't have. High frustration tolerance doesn't solve the problem. You need to make the task more doable. How can you do that?

One solution is to use your library to find articles or books that give you a simple version of the original material. Perhaps someone has summarized the philosopher's views for the general reader. Also, the library has background information about the relevant topic. If the struggle you're having is with the main text in class, look for another text on the same topic that might be more readable. You will find that almost every instructor will be impressed by such an active attempt to address a learning obstacle.

TIP 8   Compliment instructors who challenge you and refuse to treat you like a passive sponge.

Recently, we received the following as part of a note from a former student who is now quite successful:

> I want to thank you for all of your help during my undergraduate studies. As my *most frustrating professors,* I feel that you have taught me better than all of my other professors combined. While most of my other professors were teaching specific subjects, I learned from you how to think and evaluate regardless of the material.

Needless to say, such comments made us both feel good. We don't mention this note to brag about our teaching but to help make two points. First, students can experience many long-term benefits from learning to handle frustration. Second, instructors are human and enjoy getting positive feedback from active learners.

Instructors who challenge and push students and who spend a lot of time designing their classes so that their students can engage in active learning exercises frequently must endure much short-term hassle to encourage long-term learning gains in their students. Students often complain to them about too much work, or express feelings of frustration, or moan and groan a lot. Rarely do students thank or cheer the instructor for making them work hard, or for giving them long assignments, or for teaching them how to answer their own questions.

You can help your teachers and future students as well by letting them know you appreciate their effort. Remember that you are teaching professors while they are teaching you.

There are many things you can do to reinforce such an instructor. For example, you can tell him directly how much you appreciate being challenged. Or you can drop him an appreciative note during the semester. Also, active participation in class can be a form of reinforcement.

 TIP 9   Accept mistakes as a necessary part of striving for excellence.

Imagine you are learning how to serve in tennis. You make an attempt. It flies way past the box where serves are supposed to land. You make another attempt; it hits the net. But your mistakes tell you how to adjust your motion, and over time you improve. Mistakes inform you! You can't get better at anything unless you make mistakes. As an active learner, you don't want to play it safe by avoiding mistakes. Making mistakes does not mean you are a bad or worthless person. They mean that you are fallible, like other human beings, and that you need to modify something you are doing. With frequent practice, you can see the act of taking risks as a learner as one of your most rewarding human experiences.

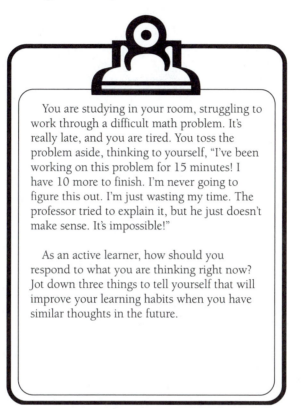

You are studying in your room, struggling to work through a difficult math problem. It's really late, and you are tired. You toss the problem aside, thinking to yourself, "I've been working on this problem for 15 minutes! I have 10 more to finish. I'm never going to figure this out. I'm just wasting my time. The professor tried to explain it, but he just doesn't make sense. It's impossible!"

As an active learner, how should you respond to what you are thinking right now? Jot down three things to tell yourself that will improve your learning habits when you have similar thoughts in the future.

QUICK REVIEW BOX

1. Focus on the long-run benefits of active learning.
2. Start small, and then take small steps.
3. Reward yourself for small improvements and overcoming LFT.
4. Challenge thoughts that promote LFT.
5. Practice "standing it."
6. Surround yourself with others who have HFT.
7. Break difficult learning activities into doable parts.
8. Compliment instructors who challenge you and refuse to treat you like a passive sponge.
9. Accept mistakes as a necessary part of striving for excellence.

PLACES TO SEARCH FOR MORE ON THIS TOPIC

Neil Postman, *Amusing Ourselves to Death* (New York: Viking Press, 1985).

Aldous Huxley, *Brave New World* (New York: Harper and Row, 1969).

http://www.eur.nl/fsw/research/happiness/ (discusses research about the need to think carefully about what makes us happy in the long run).

CHAPTER 4

RESISTING MENTAL HABITS THAT INTERFERE WITH ACTIVE LEARNING

The greatest obstacle to discovery is not ignorance—it is the illusion of knowledge.

—DANIEL J. BOORSTIN

Belief gets in the way of learning.

—ROBERT HEINLEIN

SELF-ASSESSMENT

_____ I often use evidence other than my own experience to prove my claims.

_____ I often talk to people who others view as "different."

_____ I am not satisfied with simple explanations.

_____ I understand that if I am to learn, I must work hard to change certain of my beliefs.

OBSTACLE

■ Mental habits that prevent active learning

When you meet someone for the first time, you bring to that experience a rich history. You have seen many films, talked to many people, and experienced a broad range of things. This history is a great aid in your interactions. It enables you to see what you would otherwise have missed. *But,* that same history can distort your view of the other person, giving you a quite misleading impression.

This chapter focuses on the harmful role played by particular mental habits, which can seriously distort learning opportunities. These habits are quite natural; but when you are aware of them, you can better resist their attraction as stumbling blocks to excellence.

Recency Effect

For example, one of our unhealthy mental habits is to rely much too much on our most recent experiences as a guide to future experiences. We remember them more clearly than any other information; they seem more *real.* Consequently, if you were recently in a romantic relationship with someone, and it failed, you might conclude that you do not want to go out with anyone ever again. Yet, this is probably not a sensible conclusion. There may be many other individuals with whom you could benefit greatly by becoming closer.

Or you might think you need to think seriously about buying a gun after just reading about a recent outbreak of violence in schools. But then you stop and think just how typical were those instances of violence? Do they happen all the time? After some thought, you realize the danger of highlighting recent events. Forget the gun!

Over-Reliance on Personal Experiences

Another very common mental bias is to rely completely on your own personal experiences when making decisions. Because we trust what we have seen ourselves, we often lean on these experiences as *THE* guide for our decisions. And while as an individual, you are capable of great insight, would you really want to rely on just one person's observations, even your own? Using a sample size of one (yourself) as evidence, when others may claim to have observed things differently, is very risky. Just because you receive two wasp bites as you walk in front of your apartment does not mean that the wasps are really bad this year.

Stereotyping

Stereotypes are also a very common mental bias. When we stereotype, we allege that a particular group has a specific set of characteristics. For example:

1. Japanese are industrious.
2. Young people are frivolous.
3. Women make the best secretaries.
4. Welfare recipients are lazy.

These illustrations pretend to tell us something significant about the quality of certain types of people. In reality, however, they hinder active learning. Stereotypes are unfair generalizations; they often persuade us to make unfavorable decisions about someone before he even expresses his ideas.

Over-Simplification

Many times, when we are trying to come to a conclusion, we try to over-simplify things. Over-simplification makes decisions easier. But ignoring complexity gets us into a lot of trouble.

For example, when trying to discover the basis for the crash of an airplane, a relatively simple cause like pilot error or defective brakes gives us a name for the cause; this simple answer seems to fill the bill. We think we have discovered the source of a significant problem. *But* preventing crashes may require us to think much more deeply about how the system of parts and human skill can be organized so that airplane crashes can be minimized.

Suppose we were to ask you whether drugs should be legalized? If you think of the question as requiring a yes or no answer, it appears to be a manageable question you can handle after some initial reflection.

But if we consider the question from a more thoughtful perspective, we can see there are many issues to consider. There are many types of drugs; legalization takes many forms; potential drug users are various ages; legalization could contribute or detract from many potential social objectives. The issue is complex. To respond to the issue skillfully, we must force ourselves to look beyond the simple answer.

Belief Perseverance

Another harmful mental bias is belief perseverance. This is the tendency to hold tightly to our current opinions. As a result of this obstacle, we often enter conversations with our minds made up. For example, if I prefer the Democratic candidate for mayor, regardless of how weak my rationale is, I may not listen to your reasons for choosing the Republican candidate. But this exaggerated loyalty to current beliefs is dangerous. It cannot only influence the way we make decisions, but the way we gather information to make decisions.

If you were intent on voting for the Democratic candidate, you might search only for information that supported her. But you would be ignoring information from other sources that might indicate that the Republican candidate is the better person for the job.

Identifying these negative mental habits and learning how to combat them, can move you a long way toward excellence in college.

TIPS ONLY THE BEST STUDENTS KNOW

 TIP 1   Increase your knowledge base.

A large number of our harmful mental habits result from the small size of our knowledge base. If we knew more about more events, people, and ideas, we would be less likely to engage in the sloppy thinking associated with the mental obstacles we have just discussed. The more you know about how others think and act, the harder it is to unfairly stereotype people, for example.

We are not urging you to just go out like a vacuum cleaner gobbling up facts. The best way to improve your mental processes is by acquainting yourself through reading, dialogue, and observation with many ideas and then actively probing and using those ideas in a disciplined manner. In fact, Chapters 6 to 8 are devoted to explaining how you can maximize the usefulness of the knowledge base you are acquiring. But our point with this tip is: You cannot use or evaluate evidence or ideas until you have them in your possession.

 TIP 2   Interact with people who are different from you.

It is very easy to make generalizations about people you don't know. For example, "Gina never laughs at my jokes. She's an Honors student, and everyone knows that honors students don't have a sense of humor." Stereotypes are simple and abundant. They also hinder active learning.

Active learners look at issues from several different angles. Having a diverse group of people to talk with about our beliefs and decisions can free us from the narrowness of our own perspective.

Go to places and events that you don't normally attend. If you spend a lot of time at sporting events, try going to a poetry reading or a musical concert. Listen and talk to the people at these gatherings. See what they think about the things that interest you.

Instead of surrounding yourself with people
who are exactly like you,

try meeting and speaking with
diverse groups of people.

▶ **TIP 3   Make yourself read sources that go more deeply into an issue.**

You may have read about a new form of contraception in a popular magazine, but what do reporters for *Newsweek* have to say about it? By reading more complex sources, you can get a richer picture of the effects of the new discovery.

The library's research databases are a useful source for moving beyond your personal experience. Look up a subject that you feel you are fairly knowledgeable about. Then read an analysis of that subject in a source that you have never even seen.

By picking an article out of an obscure magazine, you may get a side of the issue that has not been fully explored by other media sources. This experience should demonstrate that the issue is not as simple as it may seem and can force you to ask more and more thorough questions.

Your professors can also help you discover varied sources. When you are given an article to read, ask the professor, "Where can I find an article that is directly opposed to the theme of the article being assigned?"

TIP 4 Experiment with role playing and just using your imagination.

No doubt, there are certain beliefs that you feel very strongly about. Perhaps you feel abortion is wrong or that pornography contributes to violent crimes against women.

But what if you had to argue from the other side of an issue? For example, what if you had to argue that pornography does not harm women? What kind of proof would you use?

Forcing yourself to look through the eyes of another person is a difficult task, but it may aid you in discovering and understanding certain conclusions that otherwise you would not have considered. Try, for example, to see the world through the eyes of someone whose sex, race, economic background, religion, or culture is different from your own.

SPEED B^{UM}P 4-1

Look, I have already thought about the beliefs I have.
I don't want to become someone else.

We all feel threatened by opinions and arguments different from our own. It is not always pleasant to realize that we may have held views that we now no longer respect because we have discovered positions we now prefer.

So, this search for different points of view requires tremendous honesty, sincerity, and creativity: three characteristics essential to active learning. Avoid saying, "There's nothing I could say in support of that argument." Make yourself look and then look again. Be sincere in your quest. And above all, remember that none of the views we now hold came to us automatically at birth. We discovered our current opinions by opening ourselves to new evidence and ideas. You should fight to keep the same open-mindedness to change concerning your current beliefs. That openness is your best guarantee that you will not stagnate as a learner.

zena

zena

TIP 5   Examine old data.

Like Tip 2, this one emphasizes the need to examine various sources. Yet, this tip combats a different mental bias: our tendency to rely on information and memories that are easily retrieved as a basis for our decisions and judgments.

One way for you to stop making decisions based on the *latest* news report you saw is to look at articles that were written in the past. *Of course you also want to look at current information.* But remember that what is most recent might not be the best information that you can get. By best, we mean the most thoughtful, the most researched, and the most well-reasoned evidence.

Examine older sources and articles, perhaps those that were written before a particular event occurred. For example, if you were researching President Clinton's impeachment, you might want to examine books and articles written about the impeachment of previous presidents. Then, it might make sense to study some articles about the changing nature of public office in the 1990s as journalists become more eager to uncover the details of the personal

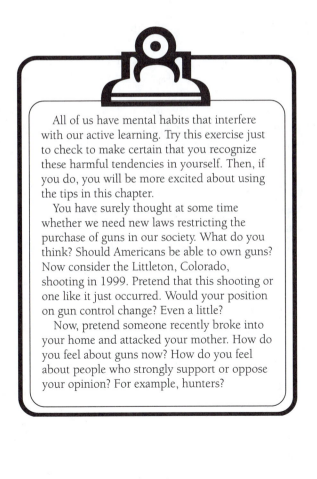

All of us have mental habits that interfere with our active learning. Try this exercise just to check to make certain that you recognize these harmful tendencies in yourself. Then, if you do, you will be more excited about using the tips in this chapter.

You have surely thought at some time whether we need new laws restricting the purchase of guns in our society. What do you think? Should Americans be able to own guns? Now consider the Littleton, Colorado, shooting in 1999. Pretend that this shooting or one like it just occurred. Would your position on gun control change? Even a little?

Now, pretend someone recently broke into your home and attacked your mother. How do you feel about guns now? How do you feel about people who strongly support or oppose your opinion? For example, hunters?

lives of politicians. After something like President Clinton's impeachment, the details and excitement of the event might distract us from the deeper truths found in relevant arguments that were provided months before the actual impeachment.

You can imagine old data as a treasure chest of ideas. These ideas can give you a fresh perspective and break current patterns of thought.

QUICK REVIEW BOX

1. Increase your knowledge base.
2. Interact with people who are different from you.
3. Make yourself read sources that go more deeply into an issue.
4. Experiment with role playing and just using your imagination.
5. Examine old data.

PLACES TO SEARCH FOR MORE ON THIS TOPIC

Daniel Kahneman, Paul Slovic, and Amos Tversky, eds., *Judgment Under Uncertainty: Heuristics and Biases* (New York: Cambridge University Press, 1982).

Magazines like *National Review, Mother Jones, The Freeman,* and *The Nation* are excellent sources of diverse opinions. In addition the Web sites for *The Wall Street Journal* and *The New York Times* often provide complex alternative points of view.

The Internet is also a robust source of conflicting opinions about almost everything. Here are a few sites to get you started:

http://www.adbusters.org/progress/links.html

http://www.alternet.org

http://www.gmt.it/pages/communitarianism

http://www.powerup.com.au/~dmcclure/progr.htm

CHAPTER 5

TAKING PRIDE IN DOUBT

It is not so much what we don't know that hurts us, as those things we do know that aren't so.

—MARK TWAIN

Some people will never learn anything for this reason: because they understand everything too soon.

—ALEXANDER POPE

SELF-ASSESSMENT

_____ I ask lots of questions before accepting conclusions from experts.

_____ I am comfortable with uncertainty.

_____ I realize that there is usually more than one reasonable answer to a question.

OBSTACLES

■ Personal need for certainty

■ Classroom emphasis on getting the right answers

To be an active learner, you must have the will to doubt. You must be comfortable with some uncertainty. When someone tells you that we won't be able to breathe in 25 years because the ozone layer will no longer be protecting us from the sun, you want to listen, but listen with your doubting impulse at ready. You need to have a "show me" attitude. Always question the answers that your teachers and your textbooks give you and seek out alternative answers. You need such an attitude for several reasons.

First, reasonable people disagree about the answers to many questions, and they can provide good reasons for their points of view. They disagree for many reasons, including how much they have considered the issue, the amount of information they have available, their values, and their biases. Rarely is any single answer to an issue so well proven that there can be absolutely no doubt about its truth.

Thus, if we don't approach conclusions with some doubt, we risk making serious mistakes. We fool ourselves into believing we already know the answers, and our contentment provides no stimulus to search for new answers. After all, if we already know, for example, what causes depression, there is no need to look any further for its cause.

Second, our conclusions are more valuable when we form them ourselves, rather than having them imposed on us by others. When we forget to question the answers given to us by others, then our beliefs are simply carbon copies of what someone else has told us to believe. We should feel best about those conclusions that we have submitted to a process of doubt. Those conclusions have weathered the questioning process to become personally established conclusions. We own them; sure, they may have originated with somebody else, but we checked closely before we made them our own.

Third, an attitude of certainty rather than doubt leads to a dogmatic learning attitude, a sense that we already have the absolute truth, rather than to an attitude of tolerance of other views. Such an attitude closes off the intellectual search in college, rather than opening it up. Certainty encourages us to impose our views on anyone who disagrees with us, rather than to strive to learn from our disagreements. By pursuing a doubting attitude, we come to realize that leaving a discussion with more questions than when we began it is a useful learning experience. We should feel proud, not uncomfortable, when we are still full of wonder.

Doubting can be very useful, but we must overcome major obstacles to achieve it. First, our minds are more prone to believe than to doubt, and they are especially prone to believe things that are consistent with our own values and beliefs. Also, we are naturally uncomfortable with uncertainty because we experience a basic need to know THE truth, to know the RIGHT answer so we can predict and control. Uncertainty threatens that need. For example, if you want to be a physician, you want to know *for sure* how to treat your patient with cancer.

Second, our teachers and our textbooks too often present information to us in a way that discourages doubt and uncertainty. Most of our tests, especially multiple choice, demand memorization of what the experts know. If we

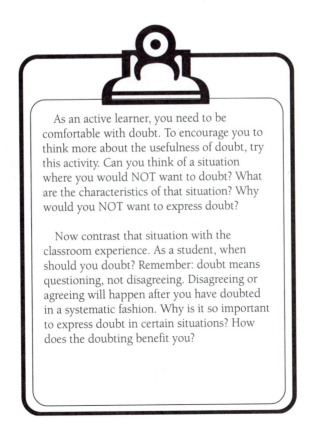

As an active learner, you need to be comfortable with doubt. To encourage you to think more about the usefulness of doubt, try this activity. Can you think of a situation where you would NOT want to doubt? What are the characteristics of that situation? Why would you NOT want to express doubt?

Now contrast that situation with the classroom experience. As a student, when should you doubt? Remember: doubt means questioning, not disagreeing. Disagreeing or agreeing will happen after you have doubted in a systematic fashion. Why is it so important to express doubt in certain situations? How does the doubting benefit you?

want to pass these tests, feelings of uncertainty and of doubt make us anxious. Our classrooms tend to be oriented to "getting the right answer," rather than to "creating good questions."

A further obstacle is that people in general tend to respect those areas of study, like physics and mathematics, that are most closely associated with certainty, and to mock disciplines, like meteorology, art and literature, that are associated with uncertainty. Thus, we come to associate respect with certainty.

TIPS ONLY THE BEST STUDENTS KNOW

▶   **TIP 1   View doubt as an essential ingredient for excellence in college.**

Remind yourself that doubt serves to keep you looking for even more learning. The contentment that comes with certainty provides no stimulus to be an active learner. Recognize that active learners want the answers of experts to arouse thought and stimulate discussion; they do not want to be told what to think. Doubt stimulates many questions, and questions stimulate further learning.

Just as a practice exercise, try to doubt what you hear in your very next class. How did it feel to be exercising the independence implied by doubting? Can you doubt, examine, and then accept? Doubting does not mean you are disagreeing; rather it means you are questioning the truth.

▶   **TIP 2   Accept reality; certainty is rare.**

Insisting that teachers and experts should have THE right answer is like looking out your window in a rain storm and demanding that the rain stop. We don't run the world!

Regardless how much we may demand certainty, we live in a complex world in which there are many things that those of us who teach can't know for sure—regardless of how many hours we have studied them. In fact, history tells us that most things that experts in our society have known FOR SURE have turned out to be disputed later in time.

"Truths" keep changing! It is easier to embrace doubt if we stop demanding certainty. Instead we need to say to ourselves, "It would be nice if experts could give me the right answers right now; but because they can't, I'm going to question their answers before prematurely accepting them."

▶   **TIP 3   Treat answers as beginnings, rather than endings.**

Think of answers to your questions as good beginnings to an interesting conversation. Answers are a start. An answer tells you that there is a question of interest to someone. But answers should not be where your curiosity ends.

Thus, for example, when a psychology expert tells you that depression is caused by a biochemical imbalance, you know that expert was trying to answer the complex, interesting question: What causes depression? You also know that *experts disagree*—often with good reasons. Knowing that experts disagree reminds you that you should have doubts about any single answer to the question. There may be other reasonable answers if you were to ask the right questions and search in the appropriate places.

By doubting any particular answer, you become part of an interesting and challenging ongoing conversation about the causes of depression. Also, although your questioning leaves you with uncertainty, it advances your knowledge because now you know much more about depression than the initial answer told you.

Think, for example, how much more knowledge you might gain by asking good questions about a doctor's diagnosis of your symptoms, or by consulting multiple doctors about how to treat some serious sickness. Remember: Doubt serves to keep you looking for more learning.

 TIP 4 **Use the library to challenge your most certain beliefs.**

When you feel really certain about something, go to the library and look for some reading that is contrary to your belief. Seek out the best arguments

SPEED B^{UM}P 5-1

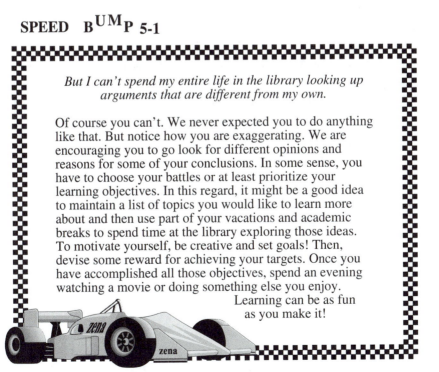

But I can't spend my entire life in the library looking up arguments that are different from my own.

Of course you can't. We never expected you to do anything like that. But notice how you are exaggerating. We are encouraging you to go look for different opinions and reasons for some of your conclusions. In some sense, you have to choose your battles or at least prioritize your learning objectives. In this regard, it might be a good idea to maintain a list of topics you would like to learn more about and then use part of your vacations and academic breaks to spend time at the library exploring those ideas. To motivate yourself, be creative and set goals! Then, devise some reward for achieving your targets. Once you have accomplished all those objectives, spend an evening watching a movie or doing something else you enjoy. Learning can be as fun as you make it!

you can find for differing beliefs. Once you see the reasonableness of those who disagree with you, you are once more in a learning mode because you then see more clearly that you need to keep learning.

   TIP 5   Take pride in doubt.

It takes hard work and intellectual courage to maintain a doubting attitude and to tolerate uncertainty. When you feel yourself asking, "Now, why should I believe that answer?" instead of just passively absorbing the answer as a certain truth, give yourself a pat on the back. You are becoming a critical thinker and an active learner.

QUICK REVIEW BOX

1. View doubt as an essential ingredient for excellence in college.
2. Accept reality; certainty is rare.
3. Treat answers as beginnings, rather than as endings.
4. Use the library to challenge your most certain beliefs.
5. Take pride in doubt.

PLACES TO SEARCH FOR MORE ON THIS TOPIC

Bertrand Russell, *The Will to Doubt* (New York: Philosophical Library, 1958).

Mary F. Belenky, Blythe Clinchy, Nancy Goldberger, & Jill Tarule, *Women's Ways of Knowing* (New York: Basic Books, 1986).

http://www.geocities.com/HotSprings/6209/ (treats "doubt" as a psychological disorder).

PART II

Knowledge

CHAPTER 6

ASKING QUESTIONS TO HELP MAKE SENSE OF THE REASONING

*One who asks a question is a fool for five minutes;
one who does not ask a question remains a fool
forever.*

—CHINESE PROVERB

To understand is to perceive patterns.

—ISAIAH BERLIN

SELF-ASSESSMENT

You walk into class. Your teacher asks you to read a small article that he thinks is especially relevant to the course. As you read to yourself, do you

    a. Look for the parts of the article that remind you of your own experiences?

    b. Ask a series of questions that are designed to discover the reasoning in the article?

    c. Attempt to memorize as much of the article as you can?

    d. Try to identify the hidden values and beliefs?

OBSTACLE

■   Not knowing how to make sense of the reasoning

Active learning begins with questioning! Effective active learners know how to ask the right questions—those questions that help them take charge of their learning and actively use their knowledge. When we know what questions to ask, we do not have to be like sponges that try to simply absorb information. Instead, we can actively make our own personal meaning out of any information we encounter.

Knowing how and when to ask particular questions gives us a sense of new power and awareness. For example, imagine reading an assignment about some recent wonder drug for lung cancer. One option you have is to try to memorize as much of the article as possible so that you could reproduce what you read when you are asked to do so. This kind of learning is useful for passing multiple choice tests and making conversation at parties.

But the active learner wants to do more. If you know what questions to ask, you can critically evaluate the information, making informed judgments about what to believe and what you need to know to better understand the meaning of the article. You can also add much to the meaning of the article by asking questions that help *make connections* between the article and other things that you know.

Not knowing the right questions to ask keeps us from being effective active learners. This chapter and the next two provide you with tips to help overcome this obstacle. It will be especially useful for you to keep in mind three kinds of questions:

    1. Questions that help you *make sense* out of the reasoning in lectures and readings.

    2. Questions that help you *evaluate* the quality of the reasoning.

SPEED B^U^M^P 6-1

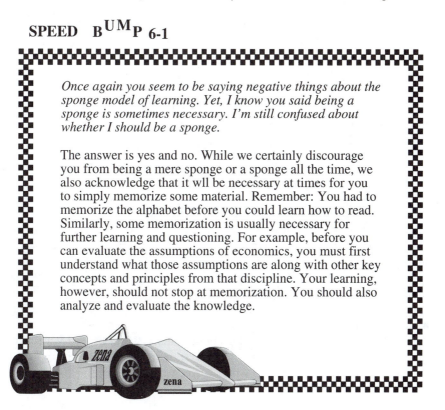

Once again you seem to be saying negative things about the sponge model of learning. Yet, I know you said being a sponge is sometimes necessary. I'm still confused about whether I should be a sponge.

The answer is yes and no. While we certainly discourage you from being a mere sponge or a sponge all the time, we also acknowledge that it wll be necessary at times for you to simply memorize some material. Remember: You had to memorize the alphabet before you could learn how to read. Similarly, some memorization is usually necessary for further learning and questioning. For example, before you can evaluate the assumptions of economics, you must first understand what those assumptions are along with other key concepts and principles from that discipline. Your learning, however, should not stop at memorization. You should also analyze and evaluate the knowledge.

3. Questions that help you *expand the meaning* of lectures and readings by making connections with other ideas and with personal experiences.

This chapter focuses on the first type of question. This list of questions is a good introduction, but active learners recognize that learning to use good questions is a lifelong process.

Tips Only the Best Students Know

    TIP 1 Always ask, what is my purpose in reading or listening to this?

Active learners recognize what their learning purpose is and ask questions accordingly. Approaching a learning task without a conscious purpose is a lot like approaching a shopping trip without knowing what you are looking for. It runs a high risk of being a complete waste of time.

Different learning purposes lead to different approaches to questioning. Here are just a few of the many reasons why you might be listening and reading in college:

- Preparing for a class discussion
- Preparing for a multiple-choice test requiring you to memorize facts
- Studying for an essay exam that requires integration of class material
- Gathering information for a research proposal
- Scanning material about a topic in which you are interested
- Preparing for a debate

The kinds of questions you ask when you critically evaluate a persuasive essay will be quite different from questions you ask when you read a textbook chapter that discusses a topic that you care little about as you prepare for a multiple-choice test. Likewise, the questions you need to ask about an article as you prepare to write a paper may be different from those you ask when you prepare for an essay exam.

How you answer the question of purpose sets the stage for how you go about further questioning. Before you dive into a learning task, always ask, What is my purpose? And *be specific* about your purpose! Stating your purpose as "study hard" will be a lot less helpful than stating it, for example, as "prepare for a class discussion in which I need to be aware of the main points and the reasons supporting them."

> **TIP 2   Ask questions that help you sort out the important parts of the reasoning.**

Active learners use questions to transform information and claims into something that is personally meaningful. They recognize that good reasoning has a structure or organization to it and that building that structure by asking questions is a first step in doing anything else with the reasoning, such as evaluating it or making connections with other things we know. Not everything that you read or hear is equally important to you. You need to sort out the most important parts and put them back together in a way that is meaningful to you.

Some parts of the reasoning are so important that they need to be identified before any other parts. Thus, you begin this sorting process by asking questions that help you find these essential parts. These very important questions are:

1. What is the issue?
2. What is the conclusion?
3. What are the reasons supporting the conclusion?

What are you asking when you ask these questions? A brief look at each should be helpful.

When writers or speakers want to convince you of something, they are *reacting* to some issue or question that is important to them. You need to know what that question is because knowing that question keeps you focused, puts the entire reasoning into some broader context and reminds you that the communicator may have ignored many possible answers.

Remember: *Answers always imply questions,* and *questions have more than one answer.*

Conclusions are answers to questions; they are what the communicator is trying to prove, the point he is trying to make. You do not know where speakers or writers are going with their reasoning until you know their conclusion. You always need to keep the conclusion in mind as you try to understand and evaluate reasoning. Questions that we can ask that help us find the conclusion include:

- What's your point?
- What are you trying to prove?
- And therefore?
- What do you want me to believe?
- What actions do you want me to take?

**Keep an eye on the purpose
and the conclusion**

Good reasoning is in the form: This, because of that. The "this" is the conclusion; the "that" is the reason(s) that make us believe the conclusion; the better the reasons, the more we should pay attention to the conclusion. Thus, to understand the basic structure of the reasoning, you need to ask: *What are the reasons?* Reasons can be in many forms, but they always provide the answer to the question:

Why do you think that is so?

Much like very curious young children, active learners are always asking "*Why?*"

▶ **TIP 3   Identify indicator words that help detect conclusions and reasons.**

Conclusions and reasons are often not obvious. Consequently, knowing clues for finding them can be very helpful. *Indicator words* are especially helpful clues. They are the words that signal that a conclusion or a reason is on its way.

Some frequently used indicator words that announce the approach of a conclusion are *consequently, for these reasons, hence, in conclusion, thus, therefore, but,* and *nevertheless*. Commonly used signals that a reason is on the way are *because, for one thing, in view of the fact that,* and *is supported by*. When you see one of these indicator words, circle it. Alternatively, you could underline reasons and conclusions in different colors or highlight the conclusion and underline the reasons. These parts of an argument are essential for any critical or creative thinking that you might do with the reasoning; so make special note of them.

▶ **TIP 4   Ask questions that help you clarify key terms and phrases in the reasoning.**

You can't fully appreciate the reasoning structure unless you understand clearly the key terms and phrases used in the reasoning. Thus, you need to study the language of the writer or speaker very carefully, asking: Are there any terms or phrases in the reasons or the conclusion that need to be clarified?

As you read, you can write in the margin:

Meaning of _____?

When you listen to a lecture, you can prepare to ask the lecturer:

Can you clarify what you mean by _____?

As a test of your own understanding of key ideas and concepts, you can ask yourself:

Can I generate another example of that idea?

If you can't produce another example, then you probably don't know what the idea means, and it needs further clarification.

Once you have identified the issue, the conclusion, and the reasons, and then clarified terms, you have put together the visible structure of the reasoning.

   TIP 5   Ask questions that help you determine hidden parts of the reasoning—the assumptions.

There's always more to reasoning than meets the eye. All reasoning takes certain ideas for granted in order for the reasoning to really make good sense. These ideas are *assumptions.* For example, when we argue that this book will be helpful to you because it will show you how to overcome obstacles to striving for excellence, our argument only makes sense if we assume

1. You can actually use suggestions that you read and
2. Striving for excellence in college is sufficiently important to you that you will make the effort required to overcome the obstacles to that goal.

Thus, to most fully understand somebody's reasoning, you need to ask:

What are the assumptions?

Finding assumptions is often hard work, and you will probably need lots of practice. One way to find them is to ask:

What did the writer or the lecturer take for granted that she didn't tell us?

Two more questions that can be very helpful are:

1. For the reasons to support the conclusion, what else must be true?
2. For me to believe the reason is true, what else must I believe?

Look for the ideas revealed by these questions when you look for assumptions. You will find that the more knowledge you have about a topic, the easier it will be to identify assumptions. Table 6.1 shows some assumptions we found in a brief argument by asking these questions. Notice that we first

TABLE 6.1   FINDING ASSUMPTIONS

Brief Essay: *Gun control laws need to be stricter. Each year nearly 30,000 Americans die from guns; the 40,000 other gun-related injuries cost America $4 billion in medical and related expenses. The need for such laws is supported by the fact that numerous associations of police chiefs and sheriffs support gun control.*

What is the conclusion?	Stricter gun control laws are needed.
What are the reasons?	1. Thousands of Americans die annually from gun, and gun-related injuries cost us billions of dollars. 2. Numerous police chiefs and sheriffs support gun control.
What are some assumptions?	1. For the first reason to support the conclusion, it must be assumed that gun control laws will succeed in reducing the number of guns available to violence-prone people. 2. For the second reason to support the conclusion, it must be taken for granted that police chiefs supporting gun control laws have some kind of special expertise about the relationship between gun laws and violence. 3. For either reason to support the conclusion, we must assume that protecting the public safety is a more important value than protecting the individual's right to bear arms.

performed the necessary step of determining the conclusion and reasons before identifying the assumptions.

➧ **TIP 6 Ask questions that help you find value preferences.**

Why do some very reasonable people charge that abortion is murder, while other equally reasonable observers see abortion as acceptable human conduct? Why is it that people who have access to the same facts on an issue still disagree after studying those facts?

The primary answer is the existence of a special kind of assumptions, particular value preferences or core beliefs about how we should see the world. Because people disagree about these value preferences, they often see the same reasoning in a very different light from someone with different value preferences. These differences in value preferences affect what reasons we respect and, thus, the conclusions we reach.

Values are ideas that people care about, think are worthwhile, or strive to achieve. For example, freedom of speech, security, and equality are all important values. But the importance we attach to values like these varies a great deal. In a clash between two values, we come to expect that some will weight one of the values as the more important, while others will reverse the emphasis. Our choices will be shaped often by the preferences we hold for one value over another.

For example, some college professors claim that having students complete classroom projects in groups is preferable to having each student work alone. It is highly likely that this conclusion is greatly influenced by a value preference that cooperation is more important than competition.

Someone's preferences for particular values will usually be unstated. Yet they will have a major influence on her conclusions and on how she chooses to behave. These unstated ideas about value preferences function as value assumptions. Some refer to these value assumptions as value judgments.

To detect value preferences ask questions like the following:

- What idea does someone care about that makes him want to argue for this particular conclusion?
- What would someone care about who would choose this particular reason or set of reasons as part of an argument?
- What values are in conflict when we are discussing this particular issue?

A good starting point in finding value preferences is to check the background of the speaker or author. Is he a businessman, a union leader, a doctor,

TABLE 6.2   TYPICAL VALUE CONFLICTS AND SAMPLE CONTROVERSIES

1. Equality vs. Individualism	1. Are racial quotas fair?
2. Order vs. Freedom of Speech	2. Should universities ban speech that is hateful?
3. Compassion vs. Honesty	3. Should you warn your friend about his bad habits?
4. Tradition vs. Novelty	4. Should divorce be easily available?

or an apartment tenant? What interests does such a person ordinarily wish to protect? Remember, however, to avoid making an erroneous assumption that every member of a group shares the same value preferences.

Table 6.2 lists some common value preferences together with controversies in which they ordinarily play a large role.

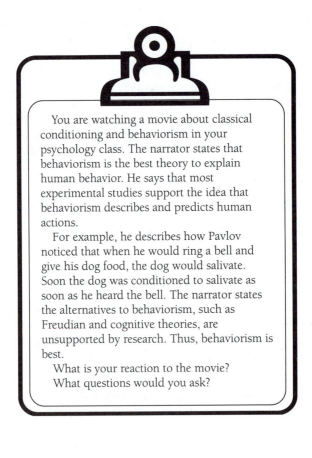

You are watching a movie about classical conditioning and behaviorism in your psychology class. The narrator states that behaviorism is the best theory to explain human behavior. He says that most experimental studies support the idea that behaviorism describes and predicts human actions.

For example, he describes how Pavlov noticed that when he would ring a bell and give his dog food, the dog would salivate. Soon the dog was conditioned to salivate as soon as he heard the bell. The narrator states the alternatives to behaviorism, such as Freudian and cognitive theories, are unsupported by research. Thus, behaviorism is best.

What is your reaction to the movie?
What questions would you ask?

Quick Review Box

1. Always ask, what is my purpose in reading or listening to this?
2. Ask questions that help you sort out the important parts of the reasoning.
3. Identify indicator words that detect conclusions and reasons.
4. Ask questions that help you clarify key terms and phrases in the reasoning.
5. Ask questions that help you determine hidden parts of the reasoning—the assumptions.
6. Ask questions that help you find value preferences.

Places to Search for More on This Topic

Theodore Schick and Lewis Vaughn, *How to Think about Weird Things* (Mountain View, CA: Mayfield, 1999).

Arthur K. Bierman and R.N. Assali, *The Critical Thinking Handbook* (Upper Saddle River, NJ: Prentice Hall, 1996).

http://www.sonoma.edu/cthink

ASKING QUESTIONS TO EVALUATE THE REASONING

The important thing is not to stop questioning.

—ALBERT EINSTEIN

It is important that students bring a certain . . . irreverence to their studies; they are not here to worship what is known, but to question it.

—JACOB BRONOWSKI

SELF-ASSESSMENT

_____ 1. I feel good because I know how to question experts.

_____ 2. I know questions to ask that help me sort out good reasons from bad reasons.

_____ 3. I often write in the margins, "How good is the evidence?"

_____ 4. I know what questions to ask about reports of research findings.

_____ 5. I am usually cautious about drawing conclusions unless they are well supported by evidence.

OBSTACLE

■   Not knowing how to evaluate

When active learners care about an issue, they are not only interested in understanding what others say to them, but also in *making judgments* about the quality or the worth of the reasoning. They want to decide whether to agree or disagree. In addition, they look for ways to improve the reasoning process. They aren't happy with memorizing what they've heard and read; they want to *evaluate* it. Evaluation is the essence of *critical thinking!*

Evaluation is extremely important because some reasoning is much better than other reasoning. Experts often disagree. This forces us to evaluate.

SPEED BUMP 7-1

If experts disagree, how can I believe anything?

You can believe those things that you have understood and then evaluated. Will you want to hold on to those conclusions for which you have evaluated the reasons and then found them strong? Yes, unless you encounter reasoning that is even stronger! Then you should change your mind as a sign of your mental openness and honesty.

Our tips in this chapter are the questions you need to ask to be good evaluators along with hints about how to ask such questions.

TIPS ONLY THE BEST STUDENTS KNOW

➧ **TIP 1   Search for any fallacies in the reasoning.**

Check the reasoning structure to see whether it includes any logical mistakes—what we refer to as *fallacies* in reasoning. There are numerous common reasoning fallacies, and many have been given fancy names. But you don't need to know all the common fallacies and their names to be able to detect them.

One of the best ways to find reasoning fallacies is to remember what kinds of reasons are good reasons—those reasons that are **believable** and **relevant** to the conclusion. It is often a good idea to try to imagine reasons that potentially might be relevant to the conclusion and then compare them to the reasons provided. If a reason doesn't look or sound relevant, there is probably a fallacy in the reasoning. Another good way to locate fallacies is to recognize mistaken assumptions, when you ask the question, what are the assumptions? Most fallacies in reasoning are caused by bad assumptions. Common fallacies include:

- Attacking a person or a person's background, instead of the person's ideas.
- Making it seem as though there are only two choices when there are more.
- Distracting our attention from the issue by getting us concerned about something irrelevant to it.
- Appealing to authorities who have no good basis for their judgments.
- Supporting a conclusion by arguing that most people are in favor of it.
- Claiming that because one event occurred after another, it was caused by the prior event.

Active learners know what good reasons are and alert to the possibility of fallacies in reasoning. A helpful way to get acquainted with different kinds of reasoning errors so that you can more easily detect them is to read *Attacking Faulty Reasoning* by Edward Damer.

➧ **TIP 2   Ask whether any evidence is provided.**

A belief or conclusion draws strength from its foundation. While you certainly should listen to whatever someone has to say, how much respect you give to the conclusion depends on the support given for it. For example, if your text makes the claim that the major cause of teenage drug use is the increase in two career marriages, you should ask, "Is there any evidence provided on behalf of that claim?" As you develop the habit of looking at the quality of the support, you will notice that far too many conclusions are provided without any evidence at all. You can spot these instances and, also, identify whatever evidence is offered by regularly asking: *What is the evidence?*

▶ **TIP 3   Ask how good the evidence is.**

Next, we should ask about the quality of the evidence. When you find evidence, you have to decide whether it is any good. You should allow some evidence to influence you much more than other evidence. For example, in deciding how to react to someone's argument, you would want to be impressed by a systematic, well-designed, large-scale research study; but you would hesitate to rely on a highly biased appeal from a single expert who has little knowledge about the issue.

To practice finding fallacies, see how many fallacies you can crowd into 3 paragraphs. Try to form an argument that looks believable, but is bursting with fallacies. The purpose of this exercise is to review the meaning and role of the fallacies mentioned in this tip.

▶ **TIP 4   Check for questionable intuitions, appeals to authority, or personal testimonials.**

Three common kinds of highly questionable evidence are reliance on intuitions, appeals to authorities or experts, and personal testimonials. All of these should be relied on only with great caution.

A major problem with intuition is that it is private; you have no good way to judge its dependability. Thus, when intuitive beliefs differ, which is often the case, you have no good basis for deciding which belief is preferable. Consequently, you must be very cautious about claims backed up only by intuition. You should ask the question: *Is there any good reason I should believe this intuitive idea?*

Although experts and authorities often have useful experience and evidence, they are often wrong and frequently disagree. Thus, you always need to ask: *"Why should I believe this authority or expert?"* Active learners try to find out as much as they can about an authority before they rely on his or her ideas. They ask questions such as:

- How much expertise or training does the authority have about this subject?

- Is this authority in a position to have especially good access to pertinent facts?
- Is there good reason to believe that the authority is relatively free of distorting influences, such as personal biases, values, or financial ties?

Don't be afraid to question the experts!

Because personal experiences are very vivid in their memories, people often rely on them to support their beliefs. However, personal testimonials by themselves are never good evidence. They fail to give you a representative sample of experiences. Also, personal testimonials tend to be highly biased and not objective. A single striking experience or several such experiences can demonstrate that certain outcomes are *possible,* but such experiences can't demonstrate that such outcomes are *typical.* Beware of arguments that say, "My experience proves . . ." or arguments that cite many personal testimonials as evidence, one of the most common kinds of evidence used in television commercials. Always ask of personal testimonials:

How selective are these testimonials?

What factors might bias them?

What possible testimonials are omitted?

Tɪᴘ 5   **Examine the quality of the research evidence.**

Research studies are usually more careful than personal observations or case studies in trying to minimize biases and thus can sometimes provide you with more dependable evidence for a conclusion; but you still want to examine the studies closely for a variety of reasons, including the following:

- Such studies vary in quality;
- Research findings are often contradictory;
- Researchers have expectations, attitudes, values, and needs that bias their research;
- Speakers and writers often distort or simplify research conclusions;
- Research generalizations often change over time, especially claims about human behavior; and
- The need for financial gain, status, security and other factors can affect research outcomes.

In brief, researchers are human beings, not computers. Questions that you can ask about research findings to help you decide whether they are good evidence include:

What is the quality of the source of the report?

Has the study been done more than once?

How selective has the communicator been in choosing which studies to mention?

Is there any reason for someone to have distorted the research?

Are there any biases or distortions in the survey questionnaires, ratings, or other measures that the researcher uses?

  TIP 6   **Search for rival and multiple causes.**

Human beings are always trying to find out the causes of things. Finding causes, however, is usually a very complex task. First, most events result from a combination of causes. Second, the same events may have different causes. Third, most research evidence that supports one cause can also be explained as the result of quite different causes. Thus, while writers and speakers will present you with evidence for *THE* cause of an event that makes the most sense to them, you need to always ask questions like:

Could anything else account for that?

What other interpretations are possible?

Might there be multiple causes for such events?

You should be especially alert to a very common problem in our search for causes. Too many people have the tendency to believe that just because one event preceded another event, the first caused the second.

For instance, suppose you take an aspirin for your headache; then several hours later your headache disappears. If you conclude that you know why the headache went away—the aspirin did it—you need to back up a minute and consider rival causes. Maybe the aspirin worked its magic, and then again any number of other factors could have affected how your head felt later.

Remember: Because communicators usually have biases about causes, you need to search out rival and multiple causes on your own. This is a very important critical thinking activity!

▶ **TIP 7   Check for overgeneralization.**

"Fraternities are sexist." "Drinking red wine reduces the likelihood of heart attacks." "Schizophrenics are violent." All three of these claims are broad generalizations—assertions about large numbers of people or things based on studying small numbers or samples. You want to be alert for claims that are much broader in scope than is fair in light of the evidence. *We can only generalize about people and things that are like those we have studied.*

Thus drinking red wine may be helpful to the hearts of some people, but not to others. If we have studied the wine-drinking habits of only a small sample of middle-aged males living on the California coast, then we can generalize only about similar males.

▶ **TIP 8   Inquire about important missing information.**

Arguments that we encounter almost never come complete with all that we would like to know before deciding their quality. Classroom information, for example, is always highly selective. Limitations of space, time, and knowledge, as well as the intent to persuade, all work together to assure that you are always missing important information.

But you can defend yourself against this condition by actively wondering out loud about specific missing information that you would like to have before you make up your mind. Thus, identify information that would give you more confidence in your eventual opinion.

For example, imagine how much better the decision of a jury could be were the jurors permitted to ask for particular forms of information that they had not been shown. All of us are frequently in similar situations; require those trying to inform and persuade you to give you what you need for a thoughtful, reasonable evaluation. Some common kinds of important missing information are:

- Definitions of ambiguous terms.
- Assumptions.
- An author's background.
- Counter-arguments.
- Potential negative consequences of what is being proposed.

Once you get used to asking these kinds of questions, you will be able to evaluate beliefs and proposed actions on your own. Often instructors will not explicitly require you to evaluate material. But once you develop the habit of evaluating, you will find the resulting sense of self-worth and independence so fulfilling that you will choose to evaluate reasoning as a regular part of your life.

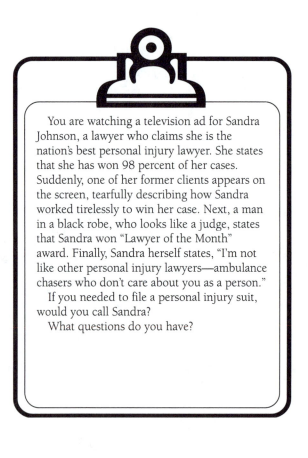

You are watching a television ad for Sandra Johnson, a lawyer who claims she is the nation's best personal injury lawyer. She states that she has won 98 percent of her cases. Suddenly, one of her former clients appears on the screen, tearfully describing how Sandra worked tirelessly to win her case. Next, a man in a black robe, who looks like a judge, states that Sandra won "Lawyer of the Month" award. Finally, Sandra herself states, "I'm not like other personal injury lawyers—ambulance chasers who don't care about you as a person."

If you needed to file a personal injury suit, would you call Sandra?

What questions do you have?

QUICK REVIEW BOX

1. Search for any fallacies in the reasoning.
2. Ask if any evidence is provided for the beliefs and claims?
3. Ask how good the evidence is?
4. Check for questionable intuitions, appeals to authority, or personal testimonials.
5. Examine the quality of the research evidence.
6. Search for rival and multiple causes.
7. Check for overgeneralization.
8. Inquire about important missing information.

PLACES TO SEARCH FOR MORE ON THIS TOPIC

M. Neil Browne and Stuart M. Keeley, *Asking the Right Questions,* 5th ed. (Upper Saddle River, NJ: Prentice Hall, 1998).

Christopher Cerf and Victor Navasky, *The Experts Speak* (New York: Villard, 1998). A collection of dozens of examples of experts' predictions that later proved incorrect.

Robert Ennis, *Critical Thinking* (Upper Saddle River, NJ: Prentice Hall, 1996).

Schuyler W. Huck and Howard M. Sandler, *Alternative Hypotheses: Alternative Interpretations of Data Based Conclusions* (New York: Harper & Row, 1979).

http://refserver.lib.vt.edu/libinst/critTHINK.HTM (bibliography for evaluating Internet sites).

CHAPTER 8

ASKING QUESTIONS THAT MAKE CONNECTIONS

Upon this gifted age, in its darkest hour,
Rains from the sky a meteoric shower
   of facts. . . . They lie unquestioned,
   uncombined,
Wisdom enough to leech us of our ill
Is daily spun, but there exists no loom
   to weave it into fabric.

—EDNA ST. VINCENT MILLAY

The world is but a canvas to the imagination.

—HENRY DAVID THOREAU

SELF-ASSESSMENT

You have several classes today—geography, biology, and golf. When you came to school, you knew you were going to get an education. But as you head to each of these classes, you wonder aloud to yourself: How are these classes providing me an education? What will you do about your question?

    a. Just wait and hope you will understand it all later.

    b. Look for similarities and differences in the courses, so that you can make some meaning from these seemingly unrelated courses.

    c. Ask your friends whether their courses seem related.

    d. Explain to yourself that your teachers and advisors must know what they are doing.

OBSTACLES

■   Not knowing how to make connections

■   Just not knowing enough to be able to make connections

The Edna St. Vincent Millay poem, written in the 1920s, is highly relevant to today's learning situation. We receive piles of seemingly unrelated information, and we need to weave it into a meaningful fabric. Active learners try to weave the information they encounter into a patterned fabric as a way to gain a deeper understanding than is possible from a sponge model approach to learning.

We encounter most information in fragments; it is in parts, not wholes. It is specific to a particular issue, or to a particular chapter, or to a particular discipline, or to particular theorist, or to a particular teacher. Our job as active learners is to approach these information fragments like weavers view pieces of fabric—something that can be put together with other pieces to form a rich and meaningful tapestry. Weavers need looms. Learners need question strategies that help them make connections. They also need to be able to locate the relevant pieces of fabric—the ideas to be connected. Our tips in this chapter are questions that can help you make a variety of different kinds of connections.

TIPS ONLY THE BEST STUDENTS KNOW

➡   **TIP 1   Ask how these ideas are connected to other ideas.**

Ideas tend to be connected in diverse ways, and the more ideas you encounter the more meaningful connections you can make. For example, it is

Questions That Help Discover Connections Between Ideas

Is this idea a part of, an element of, or a feature of something else?
Freedom of speech is an important part, or element, of democracy and of the Bill of Rights.

Are other ideas important parts of this idea?
Origins, symptoms, and prognosis are elements of the concept "disease."

Can this idea be seen as a *cause* or *consequence* of another idea?
The concept stress can be seen as being causally connected to concepts of mental health, such as depression and the Gulf War syndrome.

Is this idea an example, type, or subcategory of another idea?
Introversion and extroversion are types of personalities.

Is this idea consistent or inconsistent with other ideas?
The idea, "he who hesitates is lost" is inconsistent with the idea, "look before you leap."

Does this idea provide evidence or support for another idea?
The finding that many people grieve in similar stages supports a stage theory of grieving.

Does this idea add to or expand upon other ideas?
The theory that the cause of mass killings in schools is too much violence on television can be added to prior ideas about the causes of such killings.

Does this idea have characteristics or features that are characteristics of other ideas?
An emphasis in schools on student ratings of professors has similar characteristics to an emphasis on consumer preferences in determining the value of a product.

exciting to write in your text margins, "That idea relates to idea x, discussed yesterday," or "That idea suggests another cause for Y, which we discussed five chapters ago."

Ideas can be connected in a variety of ways. Knowing these ways gives you clues to making connections. Questions that help you make connections among ideas and examples of the kind of connection produced by that question are listed above.

▶ **TIP 2   Think about how the ideas relate to you personally.**

You care most about those ideas that relate to you personally. For example, a personality theory lecture or a lecture on supply and demand will possess more meaning for you when you can apply it to your own experiences. So, it makes sense for you to ask yourself questions like:

> How might this knowledge have an impact on my own life?
>
> Why should I personally care about this topic?

Answering these questions personalizes the information for you. It permits you to make your own meaning rather than having to rely on others to transfer their meanings to you.

   TIP 3   Ask questions that require you to seek implications and to speculate.

It is often informative to ask, so what? or, what difference does it make? Active learners are interested in asking such questions about ideas because these questions force them to imagine the consequences of ideas. They make us think deeply and creatively and increase the relevance to us of the ideas.

For example, learning that children of dual-career parents experience more frequent problems than those of single-career parents has many potentially interesting implications for how people choose to live their lives and for childcare policies.

Questions that require you to speculate about "what might have been" also make you think about the relationships among events. Asking this question provides connections that provide a much richer context for events. You can ask this question in many ways. Here are a few:

What would happen if _____ were to occur?

For example, what would happen if we make certain drugs more widely available?

What consequences would follow if _____ were true?

For example, what consequences would follow if it's true that homosexuality is a genetically determined behavior pattern?

TIP 4   Ask questions that make you connect ideas to other perspectives.

As we mentioned in an earlier chapter, ideas and reasoning reflect the perspectives, values, and belief systems of those who express them. Connecting ideas to new perspectives allows you to get a much richer picture of the ideas. For example, viewing the welfare system through the perspective of a welfare mother permits you to see it differently than perceiving it through the lens of someone trying to minimize the taxes we are paying. To encourage yourself to take other perspectives, ask:

What is another way to look at . . . ?

If I were in a different position of power, how would I look at . . . ?

If I had had very different experiences with such situations, how would I look at . . . ?

SPEED BUMP 8-1

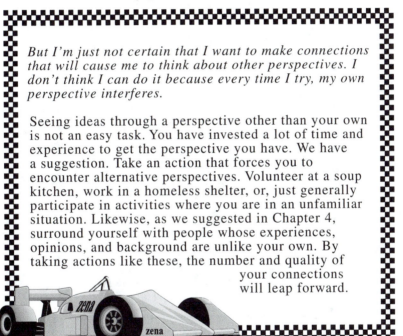

But I'm just not certain that I want to make connections that will cause me to think about other perspectives. I don't think I can do it because every time I try, my own perspective interferes.

Seeing ideas through a perspective other than your own is not an easy task. You have invested a lot of time and experience to get the perspective you have. We have a suggestion. Take an action that forces you to encounter alternative perspectives. Volunteer at a soup kitchen, work in a homeless shelter, or, just generally participate in activities where you are in an unfamiliar situation. Likewise, as we suggested in Chapter 4, surround yourself with people whose experiences, opinions, and background are unlike your own. By taking actions like these, the number and quality of your connections will leap forward.

▶ **TIP 5   Expand your knowledge base by active reading, listening, and observing.**

Internet connections expand daily. Why? New information is continually being added, and new connections among concepts are being identified. Likewise, you will be at your best in terms of making connections when you have lots of ideas and information to connect.

Your texts and lectures can give you a good start. But you can go far beyond those sources. Reading unassigned books and articles that represent diverse values, topics, and points of view, reading newspapers with varying political value preferences, and attending campus lectures can all help you add new information. The more you know, the more robust will be your connections. Engage in these activities, and you will be demonstrating your value preference for complexity over simplicity.

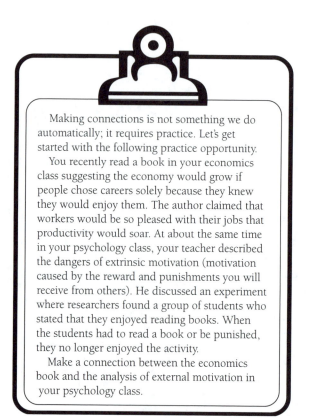

Making connections is not something we do automatically; it requires practice. Let's get started with the following practice opportunity.

You recently read a book in your economics class suggesting the economy would grow if people chose careers solely because they knew they would enjoy them. The author claimed that workers would be so pleased with their jobs that productivity would soar. At about the same time in your psychology class, your teacher described the dangers of extrinsic motivation (motivation caused by the reward and punishments you will receive from others). He discussed an experiment where researchers found a group of students who stated that they enjoyed reading books. When the students had to read a book or be punished, they no longer enjoyed the activity.

Make a connection between the economics book and the analysis of external motivation in your psychology class.

Quick Review Box

1. Ask how these ideas are connected to other ideas.
2. Think about how the ideas relate to you personally.
3. Ask questions that require you to seek implications or make speculations.
4. Ask questions that make you connect ideas to other perspectives.
5. Expand your knowledge base by active reading, listening, and observing.

PLACES TO SEARCH FOR MORE ON THIS TOPIC

Joseph Engelberg, *The Nature of Integrative Study* (Stillwater, OK: New Forums Press, 1994).

http://www.concentric.net/~Jerbob1/crehome.html (suggestions for making more creative connections).

http://www.links2go.com/topic/Creativity (links to many sites where creativity is taught).

CHAPTER 9

PREPARING FOR A CLASS WHERE ACTIVE LEARNING TAKES PLACE

The fight is won or lost far away from witnesses-behind the lines, in the gym, and out there on the road, long before I dance under those lights.

—MUHAMMAD ALI

I will prepare and some day my chance will come.

—ABRAHAM LINCOLN

SELF-ASSESSMENT

_____ I take my classes seriously, even if the course is not required for my major.

_____ I work ahead on projects.

_____ I read an assignment many times.

_____ I often talk with my friends about things I'm learning in class.

_____ I review my notes before class.

OBSTACLES

■   Inadequate preparation for class

■   Poor time management skills

College is one of the best places that you can be if you are interested in active learning. You will meet professors who will inspire you, students who can share ideas with you, and tests and questions that will challenge you. These experiences will not be as meaningful as they can be, though, if you do not prepare adequately for your classes.

Your classes can be demanding as well as very rewarding. They provide a unique opportunity to clarify confusing ideas as well as raise additional questions. But consider the following scenario:

You didn't read the assignment, or you read it once over lightly.

In this case, you will lack any in-depth understanding of the material. Thus, you will be ill-prepared to answer questions posed to you by your professor. Plus, you will be misusing the time of your instructor and the other students. Also, any comments you may offer will probably not be that closely related to the subject being discussed; and, therefore, you may lead the class in a direction that largely wastes its time. In addition, other students will probably notice your lack of seriousness, and as a result, may get the idea that classroom learning activity isn't that important. The less prepared the class is as a whole, the less opportunity there will be for productive active learning.

Active learners are people who want to learn for life, not just to pass a test. To get the most possible from your time in school, you must invest a lot of time.

Preparing well for class is not easy. This chapter provides you with a number of tips to both encourage and tell you how to prepare for a class in which active learning will take place.

Tips Only the Best Students Know

➡ **TIP 1   Read the assignment multiple times.**

Do you remember when you first came to college? No doubt you were overwhelmed by the many buildings. "How will I ever remember where everything is?" you may have thought.

Our initial encounter with something is often confusing. This theory applies to reading as well. We often become confused. We can't remember how one thing relates to another. For this reason, it will help you to read your assignments several times. As you become more familiar with the text, you will be able to put things in perspective.

And just as your confusion decreased after walking around campus a few times, so too will many of your questions be answered as you read something over and over.

➡ **TIP 2   Take notes on your assignments.**

Simply reading the assignment is not enough to effectively prepare for class, however. Over time, you will forget what you have read. Therefore, it is helpful to take notes in some systematic fashion as well.

In high school, you may have witnessed the student who, when unable to answer a teacher's question, pointed to his or her notebook and said, "But I wrote it all down!" Most likely, this student did not touch on the most important things. Our next tips should help you take notes on the most important things.

➡ **TIP 3   List the words or concepts that were most difficult for you.**

Classroom discussion works best when everyone agrees about the meaning of key terms. You can move the active learning process along by listing all the terms about which you are unsure. Looking up and writing down the definitions before class benefits you in many ways. First, in most courses, mastering the technical language is a major goal. Also, knowing which terms you do not understand tells you important questions you should ask in class. Finally, the more the class reaches agreement on important terms, the greater the chance you can avoid useless argument.

➡ **TIP 4   Write down the conclusion and reasons.**

Whether you are reading fiction or nonfiction, try to summarize the author's conclusions or main points. Then examine what reasons he or she used, or anything else that you believe might support the conclusion. Reasons and conclusions are the things you most want to remember. We have returned again and again to the reasons and the conclusion because those are the central parts of any communication.

If you are reading a story, note the various characters. Do their actions point to a general idea? Note the setting and reflect about why the author chose that setting for this scene. If you are reading an essay, try to find the reasons why the author said what he or she said. Searching for reasons and conclusions sounds basic, but it is not. *Many people fail to locate reasons and conclusions when they are told to "read."* Therefore, you should work hard to keep this task in mind all the time.

► TIP 5   Make a list of questions.

Active learning comes alive in those classes where students offer productive questions. An important part of your classroom preparation should be to list questions stimulated by your reading of the assignment. Many of the chapters in this book provide advice about what kinds of questions are especially productive.

► TIP 6   Allow yourself enough time.

Reading (finding reasons and conclusions, common themes, and basically coming to an understanding of the piece) is a time-consuming task. Therefore, when doing an assignment, allow yourself enough time. *Don't start reading an assignment an hour before class!* Give yourself the necessary time to read carefully and take notes. This will reduce your stress level and allow you to enjoy what you're reading instead of dreading it.

There are a large number of ways to *avoid procrastination*. Grandma knew something valuable when she counseled: First, you eat; then you can play. A related rule is: First, you prepare for class; then you play. The human tendency is to reverse the rule. A useful way to counter that tendency and the pressure of your peers is to systematically schedule homework assignment times, and then reward yourself in some way when you stay on schedule.

► TIP 7   Read or experience something related to the assignment.

One way you can better understand what a person has written is to read a summary or critique by someone else. Your teacher will be pleasantly surprised at your initiative. In addition, you will gain additional knowledge that you can share with the class. Eventually, others may begin to follow your example.

SPEED B^U^{M}P 9-1

How could I have the time to do all of the class preparation that you are teaching me to do? I am so busy.

The tips in this chapter are going to require time and lots of it. College students have many responsibilities. For example, if you are involved in extracurricular activities, such as sports or student organizations, those are important time commitments. Or you may have a job or family responsibilities that are competing with class preparation for your attention.

Yet, there are 24 hours in a day. A large portion of that time is available for your many time commitments. If you want to be an excellent college student, you will choose to devote some of your time to becoming a better learner.

However, you should also use some of your time to do things that you enjoy. As we have described in this book, it is possible to get intellectual meaning out of your favorite recreational activities. It is a lot of fun to ask good questions about the movies you see and the conversations you enjoy with friends. Learning can be fun, and having fun can be a learning experience.

TIP 8   Bring up classroom topics with your friends and classmates.

One goal of your education should be the application of the ideas you learn to your own life. One of the great ways you can do this is to talk to others about the subjects you learn about in class.

Discussing ideas you've learned does not have to be formal. Try to think about how a particular philosophy might influence the way you make decisions. Ask your friends what they think. If you watch a movie, take a few minutes to reflect afterwards, and see whether themes in the film relate in any way to ideas you may have encountered in class. Active learners think and talk about subjects constantly. This will help you to remember things better, as well as foster the desire to question constantly.

You will not always be in school. Good intellectual habits now will promote the desire to think and reason as you grow older.

▶ **TIP 9   Review your notes before and after each class.**

For successful active learning to take place, it is essential that you are very familiar with the subject you will be discussing. Therefore, it is important that you review your notes before class. What were the author's reasons and conclusions again? "What was the main plot or narrative?" "What are some of the questions I want to ask?" Look at your notes and try to remember all the thoughts you wrote down. This will help you in responding to questions posed by the teacher or by other students. You will also be able to raise questions of your own.

Then, because our memories tend to be very short term and we retain what we have actively organized, try to review your class notes as soon after class as possible. By studying and organizing your notes both before and after class, you move a long way toward optimal preparation.

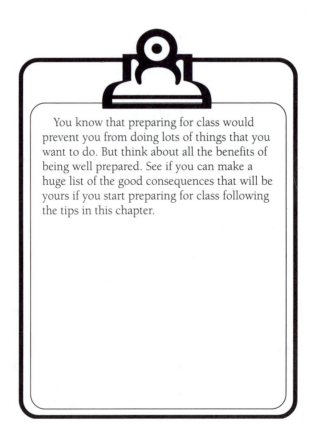

You know that preparing for class would prevent you from doing lots of things that you want to do. But think about all the benefits of being well prepared. See if you can make a huge list of the good consequences that will be yours if you start preparing for class following the tips in this chapter.

➡ TIP 10 Schedule classes carefully.

It would be ideal if you reviewed your notes right before class, so that the ideas are very fresh in your mind. Therefore, you may want to consider how you schedule your classes. If you have difficulty getting up early in the morning (and often have difficulty just making it to class on time) you might want to consider scheduling classes a little bit later. That way, you could get up, get ready, eat something, and look over your notes.

Likewise, it may be unwise to schedule classes one right after the other. If your Biology class ends at 2:20 and your Philosophy class starts at 2:30, you may have a difficult time reviewing your notes in the ten minutes you have to walk to your next class.

Many times, you will not be able to control these factors. You might have to take a course at a certain time (say the only time the required Philosophy class meets is at 2:30. In this case, you have little choice. Nevertheless, you should try your best to give yourself the necessary time you will need to be an active learner.

QUICK REVIEW BOX

1. Read the assignment multiple times.
2. Take notes on your assignments.
3. List the words or concepts that were most difficult for you.
4. Write down the conclusion and reasons.
5. Make a list of questions.
6. Allow yourself enough time.
7. Read or experience something related to the assignment.
8. Bring up classroom topics with your friends and classmates.
9. Review your notes before and after class.
10. Schedule classes carefully.

PLACES TO SEARCH FOR MORE ON THIS TOPIC

David B. Ellis, *Becoming a Master Student,* 7th ed. (Rapid City, SD: College Survival, 1994).

William Knaus, *How to Stop Procrastination* (Englewood Cliffs, NJ: Prentice Hall, 1979).

Ohmer Milton, *Effective College Learning* (New York: Harper & Row, 1964).

http://www.iss.stthomas.edu/studyguides/attmot3.htm (discussion of how to avoid procrastination).

TAKING NOTES FOR ACTIVE LEARNING

I have always thought that a man of tolerable abilities may work great changes, and accomplish great affairs among mankind, if he first forms a good plan, and . . . makes the execution of that plan his sole study and business.

—BENJAMIN FRANKLIN

The mechanic who would perfect his work must first sharpen his tools.

—CONFUCIUS

SELF-ASSESSMENT

_____ When I am taking notes, I know what is important to write down.

_____ I frequently write questions in my notes.

_____ When I reread my notes, I understand how the topics are related to one another.

_____ In my notes, I make connections between this and other courses.

OBSTACLES

■   Uncertainty about the purpose of note-taking

■   Lack of effective note-taking strategies

The reason for taking notes, according to most students, is fairly simple. You take notes because you want to do well on tests and get good grades. Furthermore, what you include in those notes is guided by what you expect the teacher to test you on.

With that purpose in mind, *you record as much as possible as quickly as possible*. When the course is over, you then dispose of your notes—they were nothing more than a study tool anyway. Many students use this passive note-taking approach—they use a sponge approach, in which they try to absorb and record as much information as they can and then "squeeze it out" after the test.

While it is important to know the information on which you will be evaluated, this "learner-as-sponge" attitude is the fundamental obstacle to good note-taking and being a learning-oriented student. Active learners want to know more than just what is required and want to be able to organize information in such a way that their knowledge tends to stay with them for long periods of time.

They may also analyze it and attempt to relate it to other experiences and ideas they have had. They use strategies for making new information and ideas useful to themselves. By this process, they personalize their notes—they make their own ideas, beliefs, and values part of their notes. Personalizing notes can help us see how the knowledge we learn fits into what we already know, helping us to make what we learn a significant part of our lives.

TIPS ONLY THE BEST STUDENTS KNOW

If you wish to get the most out of your classroom experiences, you must choose a note-taking system that promotes active learning. As a result, our approach to note-taking differs in some important ways from most others.

Our note-taking system is a two-stage process intended to help you become a more active note taker and to make your notes personal notes that you will want to keep after the class is finished. First, we offer tips that will help you *as you are taking notes*. These tips focus on:

1. *When* you should take notes,
2. *How* you should organize your notes, and
3. *What* sorts of information are important to write down.

These questions will all be addressed in the first stage.

The second stage provides you with tips that will help you *build upon and make sense of your notes,* including:

1. How to build bridges between ideas,
2. How to make transitions between topics, and
3. How to evaluate your notes.

Second stage tips help you to learn and understand your notes rather than just memorize them.

STAGE ONE TIPS

 TIP 1   **Take notes whenever you want to accelerate your learning.**

Students often believe that note-taking is unnecessary. What is the basis for such an idea? Sometimes students are confident that they will remember the information later, or they may think that notes should be taken only at certain times and not others. Both views are myths.

Myth A: My memory is so good that I don't need to take notes.

Even if you have a good memory, it is highly unlikely that you will remember the main points of a class discussion even a few hours later, much less after you have completed the class. Taking down notes provides you with an enduring stimulus for future reference. It is better to take too many notes than too few.

Myth B: When the teacher is not lecturing, it's relaxation time

When teachers decide to show a video, have students work in small groups, hold a class discussion, or design any other non-lecture activity, many students think that it is time to sit back and relax. Instead, these alternative activities provide one more opportunity to take notes.

Because students believe these myths, they often do not take notes when it would be helpful to them. Usually such activities represent important learning opportunities that should be recorded in some form in your notes like any other classroom activity.

▶ TIP 2   Adopt a Note-Taking System

You should choose your system of note taking based on your goals—what you expect to get out of your education. If your goal is to become an active, learning oriented student, then the following system will be very effective. Our system will also help you get good grades, but its primary goal is your mental development.

Next we list several suggestions for how you might organize your notes. The reasons for this particular organizational system will become clearer to you as we discuss other components of the note-taking process:

1. Keep all of your notes and handouts together and bring them with you to class every day. That way, when you attempt to integrate ideas or make connections (Tip 4), you'll have with you all the information you need.

2. Number your note pages. Again, when you integrate ideas later, having page numbers will make it easier for you to refer back to ideas from earlier in the class.

3. Write the date at the beginning of each day's notes.

4. Write lecture notes on only one side of the page. You can then use the opposite page for listing important questions, building bridges between ideas, evaluating your notes, and jotting down any ideas you may have.

5. Use some variation of outline form. While it's not necessary to use strict outline form, some approximation of it will be helpful. By writing the main points nearest to the left margin, and indenting the more specific, detailed information, you can easily keep track of the main and supporting points of lectures.

6. Save margins for comments. Your margins are a good place to comment on your notes. In margins, for example, you can indicate the teacher's conclusion and supporting reasons. You could also use that space to list questions that you have.

7. Leave a few blank spaces between topics. You want to leave spaces so that when you enter stage 2 of the note-taking process, you can fill in those spaces with a logical link between the topics. Tip 5 will focus more on making such links.

8. Keep a list of your course's core concepts or terms on the inside of your notebook's front or back cover. This will be discussed further in Tips 3 and 4. (See Figure 10.1 on pages 88–89.)

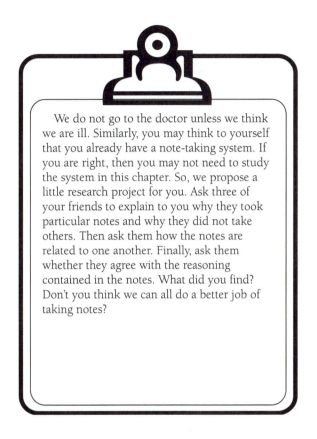

We do not go to the doctor unless we think we are ill. Similarly, you may think to yourself that you already have a note-taking system. If you are right, then you may not need to study the system in this chapter. So, we propose a little research project for you. Ask three of your friends to explain to you why they took particular notes and why they did not take others. Then ask them how the notes are related to one another. Finally, ask them whether they agree with the reasoning contained in the notes. What did you find? Don't you think we can all do a better job of taking notes?

◆ TIP 3   Focus more on meanings than words.

Focusing on words alone hinders the active student who wishes to *understand and use,* not just memorize information. Too often students try to record all of the words that the teacher says without trying to understand what the words *mean.* Instead of hurriedly writing down as many words as possible, try to understand the teacher's points and jot down the main ideas of those points, paraphrased in your own words, if possible.

For example, about every 15 minutes, jot down the two or three most important ideas that the teacher says. Try to summarize her reasons and conclusion. This practice will help you become more focused on the meaning of the teacher's lecture, rather than just the words she is saying.

Figure 10.1 Lecture Notes—History of Modern America

9/6/95

*   –   The Ford Revolution

–   Ford was 20th century hero

–   Both political parties wanted him to run for president

–   Model-T mass produced (1912)

–   continuously moving assembly line

–   cars were identical

The Ford Revolution was an early part of the technical revolution. One of first to use assembly lines. Assembly lines led to the negative effects of the technical revolution.

*   –   Technical Revolution

–   Assembly line—end "slavery" of physical labor

–   effects (causal connection)

–   physical "slavery"—mental "slavery"

–   dehumanization—machines more important than humans

–   loss of self worth—saw no finished products of their labor

Technical revolution enables the mass production of cars, which created the society on wheels.

*   –   When a society is "on wheels"

–   creation of more jobs

–   product of cars, oil

–   build roads

–   pace of life accelerates

–   communication becomes easier

–   parents have less control of children

–   dating, drive-in movies

As people began to be more mobile, many people left the country to live in the city—the urbanization of America.

9/8/95

*   –   The Urbanization of America

–   1920

–   almost 2 percent of population lives in city

–   compact living, little space

–   horses still prevalent

–   muddy roads

Figure 10.1 Continued

- 1945
    - skyscrapers prevalent
    - cities expand size
    - traffic jams
    - conditions worsen—wealthy people move to suburbs
    - concentration of poor in inner city—urban poverty
- heavy immigration
    - *The Jungle* by U. Sinclair
        - Chicago
        - conditions of poverty of immigrants
        - meat packing industry and factory work

Key Terms	Major Themes
- Continuous assembly line - mass production - dehumanization - mental slavery - geographical mobility - urbanization - immigration - urban poverty	- movement of people from rural to urban lifestyles Connection - technical revol. and society on wheels are similar Bridge - Both the automobile and the assembly line were attempts to increase human freedom. Cars - mobility frees people from their place of birth Assembly Line - free people from the difficult physical labor that machines now do.
Questions 1. How was work organized before the industrial/technical revolution? 2. Weren't people relieved to be free from the burden of heavy, physical labor? 3. Did people ever really enjoy work? 4. What does "dehumanization" mean? 5. What does she mean by "physical slavery," and "mental slavery"?	Connection - the concept of poverty in inner cities is like what we discussed in my sociology class. Bridge - Both teachers discussed the concentration of poverty in the center of the city. In sociology we talked about "concentric circles" where the poorest people lived in the inner circle of the city and the wealthiest people lived in the outer most circle of the city.

Focusing on words alone in notes can lead to memorizing words and missing meaning and significance. Passively soaking in as many words as possible can help you do well in some courses, even though you will likely forget much that you memorized moments after you have taken the test.

Focusing on meaning, however, provides many benefits that memorization cannot. When you truly understand something and connect it to your life, you probably won't forget it on the test. Further, because you have actively made sense out of it and not simply reproduced the original material in memory, you are more likely to remember it after the course is over.

SPEED B^U^MP 10-1

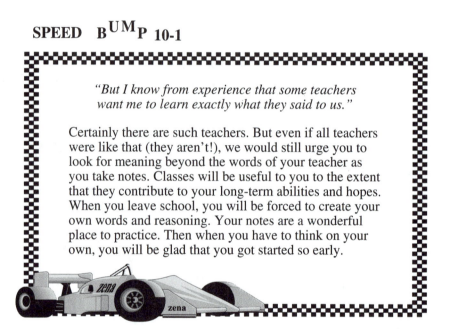

"But I know from experience that some teachers want me to learn exactly what they said to us."

Certainly there are such teachers. But even if all teachers were like that (they aren't!), we would still urge you to look for meaning beyond the words of your teacher as you take notes. Classes will be useful to you to the extent that they contribute to your long-term abilities and hopes. When you leave school, you will be forced to create your own words and reasoning. Your notes are a wonderful place to practice. Then when you have to think on your own, you will be glad that you got started so early.

To help figure out what the teacher means, you should be alert to certain words. Words (such as "fundamental," "purpose," "my point," and "crucial") should act as signals to you to listen more attentively and write the information down. These words indicate that the teacher is talking about the most important aspects of her topic. Learning to distinguish the unimportant from the important is helpful not only for test taking, but also for understanding the topic. You should also pay particular attention to the *key terms and their definitions*. These are fairly easy to identify. Look for words or phrases that teachers pronounce with emphasis or repeat. Key terms also tend to reappear frequently, surfacing regularly in readings, lectures, or class discussions.

Usually, chapters are organized around a few important ideas or concepts. These concepts, when taken together, provide a rough sketch of what the course is about. Keeping a separate list of core concepts somewhere in your notebook can help you understand the course as a whole and the individual concepts that make up that whole. The space inside the front or back covers of your notebook is a good place to keep this list.

The remaining tips on note taking are intended to help you navigate through the process of deeper learning.

STAGE 2 TIPS

➡ **TIP 4   Build bridges between ideas.**

One of the best ways that you can move from being a passive to an active learner is to learn to *search for connections* between ideas. (Chapter 8 is especially useful for this aspect of note taking.) Though it can be difficult, making links between ideas is probably the best way to help you remember ideas and to apply them.

To make the process of connecting ideas, or integration, easier to grasp, imagine yourself trying to build a bridge between two ideas. You need to find some aspect of one idea that relates to the other—those are the starting and finishing points of your bridge. Use key terms, major themes, or research studies in each section of the course, and your personal perspective to construct the bridge or connection. The skills and tips in Chapter 8 can then guide you, as a blueprint would, to construct connections in your notes.

You are not looking for a single correct connection. Many links exist between any two ideas. Rather than searching for the *right link,* your job is to search for *a single link,* one that creates a single meaning from what had been two seemingly unrelated events, ideas, or arguments.

Record these connections on the page opposite your lecture notes. Be sure to write down both the connection (they are similar, they conflict, etc.) and the bridge (the answer to the "why" question).

➡ **TIP 5   Examine your notes.**

Learning-oriented students regularly evaluate their notes. They want to stay alert to the strengths and weaknesses of the reasoning contained in those notes. The previous tips were intended to help you build your notes, generate new ideas, and relate ideas to one another. Now that you've built your notes, you should analyze and evaluate them.

Chapter 7 provides you with a set of questions to aid you in this critical thinking process. Asking critical questions about your notes and responding to them in your notes will help you understand what the teacher means when she lectures and why you should concern yourself with the information.

Approaching your notes critically enables you to evaluate the arguments in those notes and to make your own judgments about them. This process of evaluation should also prompt you to compare and contrast your notes with what you believe. Persistently ask yourself, do I agree with this, and why? Record your responses to these questions on the page opposite your lecture notes.

QUICK REVIEW BOX

1.   Take notes whenever you want to accelerate your learning.
2.   Adopt a note-taking system.
3.   Focus more on meaning than words.
4.   Build bridges between ideas.
5.   Examine your notes.

PLACES TO SEARCH FOR MORE ON THIS TOPIC

Mary Ann Rafoth, *Strategies for Learning and Remembering* (Washington, DC: NEA Professional Library, 1993).

http://www.yorku.ca/admin/cdc/lsp/note/note1.htm

http://www.utexas.edu/student/lsc/handouts/1415.html

SEARCHING FOR CLARITY IN TEXTS, LECTURES, DISCUSSIONS, AND ASSIGNMENTS

To be understood is a rare luxury.

—RALPH WALDO EMERSON

No one would talk so much ... if he knew how often he misunderstands others.

—GOETHE

SELF-ASSESSMENT

_____ When someone tells me something is good, I often ask, "Good in what sense?"

_____ I ask specific questions about how things should be done.

_____ I am quiet and attentive when others are speaking.

_____ I recognize that it is easy to misunderstand other people.

OBSTACLES

■ The belief that words have a single meaning

■ Not paying adequate attention

Words allow us to communicate our ideas to others; we may give people directions, tell them how we are feeling, or relate a humorous story. But while words often allow us to clarify things, they also bring about confusion.

For example, have you ever listened to a song and then told a friend about some meaning you took from the lyrics? If your friend is familiar with the song, he or she might have a different interpretation. The definitions that you assign to certain words in the song might have something to do with your differing conclusions.

When reacting to something like the song just described, there is not much harm in your conflicting opinions. However, in certain other contexts, confusion can cause significant problems.

Perhaps your parents have asked you to do certain chores in the past such as cleaning your room, making dinner, or taking the dog for a walk. If your father told you that you could use the family car for the night if you cleaned up the kitchen, you might be persuaded to do so. However, your idea of "cleaning" the kitchen might be very different from your father's idea of what the job entails.

For example, you might think washing the dishes and wiping the counter top is sufficient. On the other hand, your father might have had in mind dusting, waxing the floor, and other more detailed tasks. If your father came home to find that you had not completed the job to his satisfaction, he might not let you use the car. You would be upset. However, if you would have had a better idea of what your father had in mind, the problem could have been avoided.

Similar problems can arise in the classroom. As a student you might get quite angry if you misunderstand the teacher's expectations for a specific assignment. No doubt, some grades are much lower simply because the student failed to clarify the instructor's directions.

Sometimes, we don't get clear messages from our teachers and peers because we do not pay good attention. Our attention drifts. For example, many students miss instructions at the end of class because they are thinking about what they are going to do after class is over. Allowing your attention to drift is one of the most common obstacles to achieving excellence in college.

There are ways to better pay attention to and to understand what both your classmates and teachers are saying. They center on forcing yourself to pay close attention to what others are saying and then actively seeking clear definitions for the words other people use when they communicate. This chapter gives you some tips that will help prevent the frustration we all feel when we miss something important or we act on what we thought someone said, only to discover later that they said or meant something else.

Not only will a greater focus on paying attention, listening closely, and clarifying key words help your learning, but also when you pay close attention and clarify what you read and hear, you are showing greater respect for those who are trying to communicate with you. We want to be fair to others when we react to them; a reasonable starting point is *listening very carefully* and searching for what you believe they have said.

SPEED B^{U M}P 11-1

"But at some level, isn't almost any word ambiguous in many contexts? If I am right, I cannot be bothering people all the time and using every waking moment to clarify the meaning of words."

Certainly, you are right. Your points are exactly why we emphasize the importance of focusing only on clarifying certain words. The key words for you to clarify are those that have a strong effect on the reasoning. For example, any word that is used in the conclusion or reasons requires special attention. Those are the words that must be clear before you can evaluate the reasoning.

TIPS ONLY THE BEST STUDENTS KNOW

▶   TIP 1   Pay close attention and listen actively.

Many messages get sent but not accurately received because of lack of sufficient attention. As simple and important as paying attention seems, it is striking how often people fail to attend to one another. This failure is why we hear so often in our culture, "you're not listening to what I'm saying." Actually, paying close attention is a difficult process, and you need to work very hard to focus your attention and to be a good listener.

To actively attend and listen, you need to *intensely focus* on relevant input, such as the teacher's lecture or a classmate's comments. Focusing well demands the concentration of all your mental capabilities and conscious efforts to keep your mind from wandering or getting distracted.

One useful way to reduce distractions and keep focused is to keep your mind alert by getting adequate sleep and rest. Another useful strategy is to take lots of notes. Note taking requires active attending. Most importantly, you need to adopt the kind of respect for others that you would want for yourself. This attitude is one of, "I respect you enough that I want to hear everything that you have to say so well that I will truly understand it." To accomplish such an attitude, you need to push your own thoughts and needs into the background as you listen.

➡ **TIP 2   Try to restate what you just heard.**

The next time you are talking to someone, try stopping in the middle of your conversation and asking, "What is your reaction to what I just said?" You may be surprised by the response. Some people will probably have no idea what you were talking about. In many cases, however, it is unlikely that the people you talk to will fully understand the ideas you are attempting to communicate.

We need to remind ourselves of the wisdom of Emerson's observation about how terribly difficult it is for our words to be transferred to someone else without being distorted along the way. We also need to listen more closely to one another.

Instead of assuming that you know exactly what your teachers intend, try asking when something particularly important has just been said, "I'm going to repeat what I heard you say; please tell me whether I've got it right." While you may have thought that you understood perfectly, you may have been attaching or forming *your own* meaning. By double-checking with people, you will find that you frequently hear what, they believe, they never said.

➡ **TIP 3   Ask questions to clarify words that have more than one meaning.**

Have you ever taken a class because someone told you the teacher was really "good"? You might have gone into the course very excited. You also may have been disappointed when the class didn't turn out to be the way you thought it would. What happened?

One possible explanation has to do with the ambiguity of certain words. We all regularly use ambiguous words like good, bad, and interesting to describe things. These words, however, can have many meanings.

While you need to clarify these words when you use and hear or read them, doing so does not mean that every time you hear a word that has more than one definition you shout, "What do you mean by that?" But particularly when someone is trying to get you to do or believe something that has importance to your life, it is helpful to have a clear understanding of his or her reasons.

Just as asking your parents what they mean by "cleaning" the kitchen makes sense on many levels, working to clarify assignments, lectures, and explanations will help you achieve excellence in college. When you are genuinely interested in getting a clearer idea about another person's ideas, ask them questions. For example, if a classmate tells you she read a good book, ask her, "Do you mean it was especially entertaining or that it presented ideas that you just cannot get out of your head or something else entirely?"

Because so few of us have formed the habit of seeking clarification of ambiguity, you need to be careful in asking these questions. You don't want to give the impression that you are trying to annoy someone who is interacting with you. With experience, you can ask clarification questions in such a way that your behavior will be seen as an honest attempt to be an active learner. Maybe your behavior will even improve the learning habits of those you question, as they experience firsthand your curiosity and drive to really understand.

Questions like those just described can help you get a better picture of what someone else is saying. You may find it helpful to actually use the phrase "in the sense that" to clarify your ideas as well as clear up any ambiguity in other's thoughts. Whenever you come across words like "good" or "bad" or any other word or phrase that is ambiguous, you can ask, "Do you mean bad *in the sense that* the pie was too sweet, or bad *in the sense that* its crust was not flaky?"

➨   **TIP 4   Read other sources.**

When reading materials for class, you can avoid misunderstanding ambiguous ideas by taking a look at other works by the same author.

While there are certainly multiple ways to read and interpret things, an author will often have a specific or core idea in mind. For example, B.F. Skinner, a behavioral psychologist, believed that human behavior is almost exclusively the product of our environment. For you to say that B.F. Skinner believed that people have the ability to make choices that are not influenced by their environment would be unfair to Skinner.

If, in your text, you stumbled over a reference that Skinner made to humanity's lack of "freedom," you could clarify what he meant by this claim by reading something else by Skinner. You would then see this theme discussed over and over again in his work. You could be relatively certain that you now know what Skinner believes.

In addition, you can also read criticisms of someone's work by another author. This approach may provide you with a general summary of what the author is saying. Although reading criticisms of someone's thoughts is helpful in clarifying ambiguity, it is certainly a poor substitute for having a look yourself at what the author had to say; it's just one way to get started with your search.

Textbooks frequently fail to define key concepts clearly. Thus, one more way to clarify ideas is to seek out other texts that stress the same concept; see whether their definition might be clearer.

One of the hardest parts of clarifying the meanings of words is to think of alternative possible meanings. Let's have some fun. Let's take a really common word, "love," and see how many different meanings of "love" you can list. Would you be able to tell which of those meanings someone intended were he to say, "I love you."? Why would it be a good idea to clarify what he meant?

QUICK REVIEW BOX

1. Pay close attention and listen actively.
2. Try to restate what you just heard.
3. Ask questions to clarify words that have more than one meaning.
4. Read other sources.

PLACES TO SEARCH FOR MORE ON THIS TOPIC

M. Neil Browne and Stuart M. Keeley, *Asking the Right Questions,* 5th ed. (Upper Saddle River, NJ: Prentice Hall, 1998). See the chapter discussing ambiguity.

Gerald Egan, *The Skilled Helper,* 5th ed. (Pacific Grove, CA: Brooks/Cole, 1994). Especially helpful is chapter 5's discussion of attending and listening.

John Kim, *The Art of Creative Critical Thinking* (Lanham, MD: University Press of America, 1994).

http://owl.english.purdue.edu/Files/116.html

PART III

External Conditions

FINDING PEERS WHO RESPECT ACTIVE LEARNING

If you set out to be liked, you would be prepared to compromise on anything at any time, and you would achieve nothing.

—MARGARET THATCHER

No person is your friend who denies your right to grow.

—ALICE WALKER

SELF-ASSESSMENT

You have been extremely busy this semester. The more active you become as a learner, the more time it takes. For example, you are asking questions in class and meeting with your professor when you run into problems. You have been spending lots of time preparing for class. You are particularly proud of yourself for having gone to the library to find additional information for several of your classes. However, your roommates have been teasing you because you are spending so much time on your coursework. You are frustrated with their teasing because you are very excited about what you are learning through your hard work. Do you

a. Decide that your roommates are right? You have been much too serious this semester.

b. Ignore their teasing? You can't help it if they aren't striving for excellence.

c. Start to look for new roommates?

d. Explain to them why you are spending so much time on your schoolwork and encourage them to join you?

OBSTACLE

■ Peer pressure to be a passive learner

Being an active learner isn't easy. Critical thinking, being active in the classroom, and asking yourself and others good questions is both difficult and time consuming. And being an active learner can often be a lonely enterprise. Sometimes, one of the most difficult parts of being an active learner is finding other people like yourself who you can talk to and grow with.

Most people choose friends who are like themselves. If you are interested in athletics, drinking, or music, you probably have friends who share those interests. Because you share common interests and behaviors, you act as one another's support system. You reinforce each other's behavior. Whatever your interests—athletics, music, socializing, or being an active learner—you are likely to want a support system.

Finding people who share learning-oriented interests and behaviors—reading books, thinking about and discussing ideas—may require an active effort on your part. And though it's not absolutely necessary to spend time around active learners like yourself, discussing the thoughts and ideas you have is often as enjoyable as coming up with them. And sharing thoughts with others is one of the best ways to clarify and expand your ideas.

How do you go about finding people who share your appreciation for excellence in college? This chapter will attempt to answer that question.

TIPS ONLY THE BEST STUDENTS KNOW

   TIP 1   Start with realistic expectations.

First, and above all, you must realize that you live in a society that has many exciting distractions that stand in the way of active learning. Consequently, when you begin searching for other active learners, you'll notice right away that some people, for whatever reasons, are simply not interested in being an excellent learner.

   TIP 2   Choose your classes carefully.

Classes are one place where you could potentially meet learning-oriented peers. So choose classes carefully; active learners will often flock to professors who mentally challenge their students. While other students are trying to avoid these professors, you may want to seek them out because of the excellent learners you may meet in such classes.

Whenever you are in class, listen carefully to your peers and study their behaviors. Those who ask thoughtful questions, raise their hands frequently, or listen closely to the professor (all things that you should be doing regularly) are probably themselves trying to be active learners.

   TIP 3   Go to places that attract active learners.

People who enjoy reading and thinking about ideas often spend time in similar places: libraries, bookstores, and coffee shops (or places where a lot of discussion occurs). By spending more time in these places, you can meet and talk with some of these people.

An excellent way to meet learning-oriented people is to get a job in one of these places. If, for example, you worked in the library on weekend evenings, the people in the library at those times are probably especially excited about active learning.

   TIP 4   Attend academic and cultural events.

Universities and organizations typically sponsor many activities intended to broaden cultural awareness and enrich student experiences.

Invited lectures are a good example. Several departments and university organizations sponsor lecturers to speak on a range of topics. Lectures can benefit you both because you may meet people there and because you can learn something new.

Organizations often sponsor a variety of diversity awareness programs. Because these are frequently well attended, and because they generally offer alternative perspectives for understanding (American) culture, they are excellent places to meet other people with more active and open minds.

▶ **TIP 5 Work to build active learning habits in your current friends.**

You need not wait around to discover active learners; you may be able to create new ones from among your current friends. Many students are not active learners. Perhaps they have not been taught or have simply not experienced the value of learning, or maybe they have decided that learning is not one of their higher priorities.

You can provide encouragement and suggestions that can move them more in your direction. Active learning behaviors make you stand out from some of your peers. You have different values and you behave differently. When

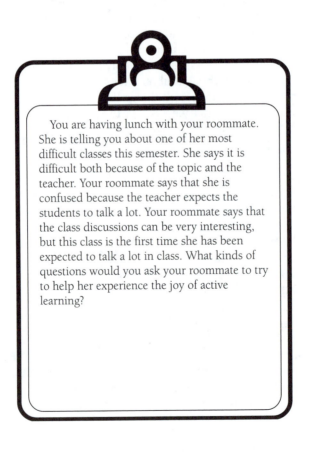

You are having lunch with your roommate. She is telling you about one of her most difficult classes this semester. She says it is difficult both because of the topic and the teacher. Your roommate says that she is confused because the teacher expects the students to talk a lot. Your roommate says that the class discussions can be very interesting, but this class is the first time she has been expected to talk a lot in class. What kinds of questions would you ask your roommate to try to help her experience the joy of active learning?

your friends note these differences, seize the opportunity to explain what you see and understand only because of those differences.

As you participate in classes and events, you have the potential to help your peers. Though you should not expect immediate success, sometimes a love for learning can be contagious. Some people truly would like to be active learners, but don't know how to go about it; they may not have anyone who can serve as an example of active learning. By sharing your enthusiasm for learning, you may be able to help other people learn to appreciate what you have learned to appreciate.

QUICK REVIEW BOX

1. Start with realistic expectations.
2. Choose your classes carefully.
3. Go to places that attract active learners.
4. Attend academic and cultural events.
5. Work to build active learning habits in your current friends.

PLACES TO SEARCH FOR MORE ON THIS TOPIC

Ivar Frones, *Among Peers: On the Meaning of Peers in the Process of Socialization* (Oslo: Scandinavian University Press, 1995).

Lawrence Steinberg, *Beyond the Classroom* (New York: Simon & Schuster, 1996).

ADJUSTING TO PROFESSORS WHO SEEM NOT TO ENCOURAGE ACTIVE LEARNING

The world of knowledge takes a crazy turn
When teachers themselves are taught to learn.

—BERTOLT BRECHT

Those who know how to think need no teachers.

—MAHATMA GANDHI

SELF-ASSESSMENT

Last semester you enjoyed engaging in several active learning behaviors. You were actively participating in class, and your note-taking process greatly improved. Your ability to recognize and evaluate arguments improved because of your practice in a few of your courses. However, you are unsure that you will be able to use your active learning skills in your history course this semester. Your teacher simply puts an outline on the overhead projector and begins lecturing. He doesn't seem to respond favorably to questions; he briefly answers the question and rushes back to his lecture. You are disappointed in the course. Do you

a. Drop it? You want to take a class where active learning is encouraged.
b. Decide that you will be a sponge in this course and practice your skills in your other classes?
c. Practice your active learning skills as best you can?
d. Talk to the teacher outside of class? He might be more willing to respond to questions outside of class.

When you find yourself in a classroom that you believe is not helpful to active learning, it is especially important to check and recheck your perception. You want to make sure that you've taken certain steps before you make a final decision about your professor's commitment to active learning.

Being a professor is an occupation. As is the case with other occupations such as dentists, lawyers, secretaries, and construction workers, some professors are better than others. Professors in general very much want you to be an active learner; the dream of a society of active learners may be the major reason they chose to teach.

Yet, there are times when certain professors may not seem to care. If you find yourself in this unfortunate situation, one thing you can do is drop the course. Such action would allow you to seek out those professors more beneficial to your learning experience. But the drop option is not always workable. You might need to take a particular course to graduate. Or, there may not be another course available that fits both into your class schedule and your program of study.

In these instances, you will have to interact with a professor who appears to be more an obstacle than a helping hand to your active learning. This chapter will help you to keep your learning active in such a situation.

Obstacle

■ Teachers who appear to discourage active learning.

There are at least three different kinds of professors whom you might see as an obstacle to active learning. First, there is the professor whose personality is such that it is difficult "to read" him or her. For example, your professor might be a shy person who has difficulty interacting with others. As a consequence, even though he believes himself to be engaging his students in active learning, this effort may not be visible to the students themselves. Let's call this professor "the Tentative Professor."

The second type of professor who might be an obstacle in your push for educational excellence is what we'll call "the Disillusioned Professor." She is enthusiastic about active learning but believes that it's nearly impossible. In the past, she has attempted to promote active learning but has met strong student opposition on each occasion. As a consequence, she has abandoned active learning, believing students to be either unwilling or incapable of what this book is encouraging.

The third kind of professor who might be an obstacle to you is the type who emphasizes your reproduction of lectures and text as his learning goals. Unlike the Tentative Professor and the Disillusioned Professor, this type of professor has chosen to create a classroom environment in which the teacher is an active dispenser of knowledge, while the students' role is to accumulate that knowledge. We'll call this type of professor "the Knowledge Dispenser Professor."

TIPS ONLY THE BEST STUDENTS KNOW

What you want to do to improve your experience in nonactive learning environments depends on the type of professor with whom you are dealing. Consequently, the tips that follow include a note designating whether they refer primarily to the Tentative, Disillusioned, or Knowledge Dispenser Professor.

▶ TIP 1   Put yourself in your professor's shoes.

There are a number of reasons why professors of any type might be less than enchanted with students. Professors can't help but notice that many students seem to lack interest in the learning experience. There are more than a few students who come to class unprepared, turn papers and homework assignments in late, and have a general disregard for the joy and rewards of active learning. In addition, students complain about workloads and express concern for only those facts and ideas that are going to be on the upcoming test. Taken together, these behaviors can suggest to the professor that students merely want to get through a course with the least possible work.

If you are aware that many professors have these perceptions of students, then you will be better equipped to deal with both the Tentative and

Disillusioned Professor. First, this recognition provides you with a greater understanding of the professor's intentions, which in turn can help you respond with feelings more positive than anger and disappointment.

Additionally, with such recognition, you can make a conscious effort not to act as other students are acting. Taking this step is extremely important. You can help create the professors you need. If the Disillusioned Professor is ever going to restore her faith in students, then she needs to see that there are exceptions to her generalizations about them. Likewise, a Tentative Professor is likely to gain confidence to better pursue active learning after he sees that not all students are opposed to educational excellence.

▶ TIP 2   Shape your learning environment.

Attempting to shape the classroom environment can be of great benefit to both interactions with your professor and the overall functioning of the classroom. "But," you say, "I am only a student! And besides, as a student, I'm but one among many. How am I supposed to have any impact on how my class operates?!"

So what can you do? One thing you can do is set an example for other students while expressing your interest in active learning to the teacher by asking questions in class. To do this, you'll need to do your course reading carefully. After all, good questions can't be formulated out of thin air.

SPEED B$^{U M}$P 13-1

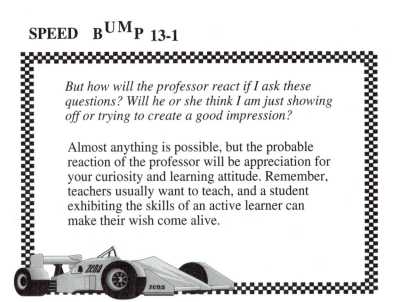

But how will the professor react if I ask these questions? Will he or she think I am just showing off or trying to create a good impression?

Almost anything is possible, but the probable reaction of the professor will be appreciation for your curiosity and learning attitude. Remember, teachers usually want to teach, and a student exhibiting the skills of an active learner can make their wish come alive.

Also, it's probably a good idea to make sure the questions require complex answers. A main reason you're asking the question is to help create a classroom environment in which both teacher and students are active participants. If your question can be answered in one or two words, that allows the teacher to return to lecturing and the other students to continue being passive.

Asking good questions in class can help demonstrate to the Disillusioned Professor that there is at least one student in her class who takes a great interest in learning. In addition, questioning can help the Tentative Professor more easily reach out to his students, because he will have the confidence that some students want an active learning environment. Finally, taking this action might draw other learning-oriented students out of hiding.

A second step you can take goes beyond what we discussed in Tip 1. You'll recall that we encouraged you to avoid harmful student behavior. You can do even more to shape your classroom environment. When a professor asks tough questions or assigns challenging work only to be met by a chorus of complaints, try defending the professor.

There are tactful ways to defend your professor's attempts to make the classroom more challenging and interactive without setting your peers against you. For example, you can attempt to quiet the collective groan by asking questions about the assignment in a manner that demonstrates your enthusiasm. Taking actions such as these can really help the Tentative Professor. In addition, you might draw out students who also are anything but disappointed with a challenging question or assignment.

◆ TIP 3   Reach out to the professor.

Reaching out to the Tentative Professor may encourage him to be more interactive, an element essential to an active learning environment. Similarly, reaching out to the Disillusioned Professor in a way that expresses interest in ideas may help restore her faith in students. Reaching out to the Knowledge Dispenser Professor may enable you to take advantage of someone who may be a rich source of ideas for you.

One of the easiest ways to extend a learning-oriented hand to your professor is to approach the professor after class and ask him for extra reading related to the course material. For example, you might ask your professor where you could find a criticism of a particular idea or theory that you have encountered in your course reading. Alternatively, you might ask for a source that provides a more thorough treatment of a concept from the course.

Another step you can take to reach out to your professor is to pay a visit to her office. However, this should not be a visit in which you stop by just to chat. Instead, prepare a thoughtful and important question having to do with the course material. Then you and the professor can discuss the question in-depth. This out-reach on your part can be especially effective with a shy professor, because the social demands of the meeting are not great.

Yet another way to reach out to your professor probably requires the most effort but also might yield the greatest pay-off. Your professor is both a teacher and a scholar. Recognize this fact and seek out the part of his academic interests that does not come out in class, namely his writing and reading. If you find something that interests you, make it a point to engage your professor in a discussion about the particular article or book.

▶ **TIP 4   Seek out other active learners in the class.**

If you're disenchanted with your professor's neglect of active learning, you are probably not alone. Consequently, a good source for creating and sustaining active learning in such a class is other students.

To identify those students interested in active learning, begin by reflecting your own frustrations. Think about how these affect your behavior in class. Now, look around the room during class. Those of your peers who exhibit similar behaviors may be doing so because of the very same frustrations.

For example, if somebody has tried on occasion to ask the professor thoughtful questions only to be disappointed, then he might be interested in a more substantial engagement with the ideas of the course. Seek him out and find out if this is the case. If it is, then attempt to start discussions with him that will allow both of you to take a more active approach to learning the course material.

By talking outside of class, even if only briefly, you will get the opportunity to have some active engagement with the course material. You and your fellow active learner can compare reactions to the readings and lectures and analyze both in terms of their quality. This dialogue will permit you to have some active involvement with the class material.

▶ **TIP 5   Stay active during lectures.**

In situations where the professor predominantly lectures, it is important that you stay active during these lectures. One form of productive activity is the note-taking strategy of Chapter 10. Staying active during lectures means paying close attention but not treating your professor's words simply as truths to be memorized. You can do this by taking the proper frame of mind with you to class. It would be easy to transfer almost unthinkingly the words of your professor to the paper in front of you. However, if you want to keep your learning active, then you must resist this temptation.

A good method of resistance is to go to each and every class with the intention of critically assessing what your professor says. It might be helpful to keep in mind the questions discussed in Chapter 7 of this book. In fact, you may want to bring a list of them with you to class. Asking yourself these questions will keep your learning more active by constantly challenging you both to follow and to assess your professor's reasoning.

To aid you in doing this questioning, you may want to keep an extra notebook. In this notebook, you can record a list of questions and concerns about what was said in class. Then, you can address these questions and concerns by talking either to the professor or to other classmates or by further reading.

▶ **TIP 6   Do extra reading on your own.**

If your professor doesn't create much opportunity for active learning, you can use other active learning skills to encourage some yourself. For example, by finding related readings at the library and using such readings to make connections in the class, you can model active learning for the professor and your peers. In a sense, you can be your own professor. Find materials that clarify, supplement, disagree with, or provide new perspectives on classroom material.

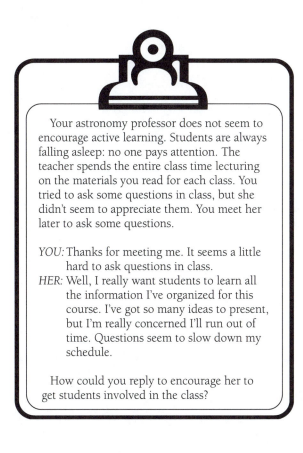

Your astronomy professor does not seem to encourage active learning. Students are always falling asleep: no one pays attention. The teacher spends the entire class time lecturing on the materials you read for each class. You tried to ask some questions in class, but she didn't seem to appreciate them. You meet her later to ask some questions.

YOU: Thanks for meeting me. It seems a little hard to ask questions in class.
HER: Well, I really want students to learn all the information I've organized for this course. I've got so many ideas to present, but I'm really concerned I'll run out of time. Questions seem to slow down my schedule.

How could you reply to encourage her to get students involved in the class?

QUICK REVIEW BOX

1. Put yourself in your professor's shoes.
2. Shape your learning environment.
3. Reach out to the professor.
4. Seek out other active learners in the class.
5. Stay active during lectures.
6. Do extra reading on your own.

PLACES TO SEARCH FOR MORE ON THIS TOPIC

Michael Moffatt, *Coming of Age in New Jersey: College and American Culture* (New Brunswick, NJ: Rutgers University Press, 1989).

http://books.mirror.org/gb.home.html (a terrific source for giving you a sense of where you might want to start should you decide to do some reading on your own).

CHAPTER 14

DISCOVERING MULTIPLE PERSPECTIVES

People only see what they are prepared to see.

—RALPH WALDO EMERSON

SELF-ASSESSMENT

_____ I notice that intelligent people differ in their beliefs about the world and disagree about what actions should be taken.

_____ I recognize that all of us, including professors and those who write text books, think, speak and act from a particular perspective.

_____ When I encounter conflicting points of view, I do not decide right away that one is "correct," while the rest are "wrong."

_____ I am suspicious of those who want to give me "the truth."

_____ When somebody says they are giving me "the facts," I wonder not only about the quality of those facts but also whether important facts have been neglected.

OBSTACLES

■ Knowing only one or two perspectives

■ Thinking with certainty that our perspective is the right one

There are many ways to look at almost everything that is significant in our lives. You can see this variety by the diversity in viewpoints among your professors, your texts, the news media, and members of Congress. One senator wants to raise taxes; another wants to lower them. One text stresses the genetic causes of violence; another stresses the breakdown of the family.

Why all this disagreement? Perhaps the most important reason is the existence of multiple perspectives or "lenses" through which people experience the world. Humans do not share a vision about what a good life is, how we should live, what is important to study while we live, or what various events in our world mean or prove. Instead, they disagree among themselves about these most significant of questions. Our way of looking at life and its purpose forms our perspective, something that guides us as we see, hear and speak.

As a learning sponge, you have little control over what you learn—that is, what you accept or reject as being true. Rather than deciding to accept or reject, sponge-oriented leaders nod "yes" to everything. Constant concern for multiple perspectives reminds us of how selective most information is and to wait before deciding what to believe or how to act. Such concern makes us want to ask, have we found and listened to multiple perspectives about this issue?

Our task in this chapter is to activate your learning by broadening your vision. As you become more aware of multiple perspectives, you will be amazed at the rich possibilities from which you can increasingly choose. Your study of multiple perspectives enlarges the range of decisions you can make. Once you know about optional viewpoints, you can evaluate them and decide for yourself what to believe or what to do, rather than just accepting as truth whatever people tell you, or just as bad, rejecting all viewpoints as unimportant.

Once you begin to see that every viewpoint is one among many possible viewpoints, then you'll no longer feel the frustration of seeking, but not finding, one perfect conclusion—the Truth. It's probably best that you give up that search anyway, because as Einstein once said, "Those who make claims to holding Truth and knowledge are shipwrecked by the laughter of the gods." It's better that you keep your ship afloat.

Without constant work on our part, we tend to accept what we hear or read without questioning it. This blind acceptance of the truth is dangerous for two reasons. First, it makes you dependent on the last expert that you encountered, rather than on your own active thinking. Second, sponge-like acceptance of viewpoints increases the likelihood that you will be both confused and frustrated when you encounter conflicting points-of-view. By focusing on the search for multiple perspectives, you will naturally run into differing conclusions. They will be unavoidable.

SPEED B^U^MP 14-1

Knowing that there are many perspectives seems overwhelming. How many should I look for? Will I ever be finished? Maybe I should never have any opinions of my own because I will always need to take another look through the eyes of a different perspective.

What powerful observations! We know exactly what you mean. We have the same questions. But remember that learning excellence does not mean perfection. All any of us can do is just try to improve. There will always be new perspectives for us to examine. But meanwhile, we have decisions to make and a personal identity to create. The spirit of looking for new perspectives can help us do a more thoughtful job of doing both. We don't want to allow the huge scope of the journey to find multiple perspectives to keep us from our more immediate task of forming beliefs and commitments.

zena

zena

If you want to develop your awareness of and attention to different perspectives, you need to know three things about multiple perspectives: (a) what causes them to exist, (b) what they look like, and (c) where you can find them. The following tips deal with each of these in turn.

TIPS ONLY THE BEST STUDENTS KNOW

▶   TIP 1   Understand that an expert has a perspective.

There are several reasons why a professor or author has a certain perspective. First, not everybody in a discipline is trained exactly the same way. Take psychology for example. Some psychology professors have been trained in the tradition of Sigmund Freud, others in the tradition of B.F. Skinner, and still others in the tradition of Jean Piaget.

You don't need to know what characterizes these different schools of psychology to grasp what's significant about this process. Freud, Skinner, and Piaget each took a different approach to psychology. As a consequence, a psychologist trained in the Freudian tradition will probably have a different perspective from one trained in Skinner's way of thinking.

Professors also get their individual points of view from their values, which like yours, have been shaped by many forces, including family habits, religion, and early schooling. These values help shape their visions of what the world *is* like and *should be* like.

For example, suppose two physics professors are scheduled to talk about nuclear power to a group of science students. The first one, Fred, who has had a life-long interest in protecting the environment, feels very strongly that we should stop using nuclear energy immediately. The other professor, Marie, who has a very strong faith in the benefits of technology, is a strong supporter of nuclear power. Don't you think that Fred and Marie's lectures on nuclear power might be very different? Fred and Marie will look at the question of the use of nuclear power from different perspectives.

▶   TIP 2   Be aware that facts don't speak for themselves.

It's hard enough to recognize the impact of perspectives when experts disagree. It's even tougher for you to discover multiple points of view when either your professor or your text suggests a fact or a set of facts. After all, aren't "the facts" real and certain in a way that a perspective is not?

The answer to this question is "not exactly." Facts do not speak for themselves. Somebody has to observe, select, state, organize and interpret information before you encounter it as "the fact" or "the facts." In doing so, the person's own perspective counts.

It is important for you to distinguish between the concepts of fact and opinion. As we use the terms (shaped by our perspectives!), we view opinion and fact on a continuum. Beliefs unsupported by *any* evidence are *mere* opinions. The more evidence that supports a belief, the more that belief then becomes a fact—a well-supported opinion. Also, the more beliefs depend on evidence that is selective and subject to multiple interpretations, then the more we need to worry about the factual status of such beliefs. We need to be most concerned about just how factual beliefs are when people discuss or write about the *meaning* and the *causes* of events. We illustrate the problem of meaning in the following example:

Prosecutor Marcia Clark presented closing arguments in the O.J. Simpson case in the fall of 1995. Her actual words were the "bare" facts. But *USA Today's* reporting of experts' reviews of her argument reveals the kind of "multiple facts" that emerge when we try to interpret the meaning of such events.

- Review by university law professor: "The day has ended for the prosecution far better than it began. They have scored some of their main points with the jury."

- Review by former Los Angeles County District Attorney who prosecuted Charles Manson: "I was hopeful for superb arguments. So far it's been disappointing to me. . . . She is arguing guilt. She is doing a decent job, but I don't get the sense that her logic is so powerful that the jury feels they have no choice but to convict.

- Review by lawyer for beating victim Rodney King's civil suit: "She has done a very strong, very professional job. In terms of jumping out of the gate, she wasn't on this morning, but she got into a little more emotion in the afternoon. The tapestry she has stitched, the triangle of his blood and the victims in three different locations, was very compelling. . . ."

- Review by Los Angeles defense lawyer: "I wasn't riveted to my seat. What she's doing is, someone said this, someone said that. That's not what the jurors want to hear. They're saying "tell us a story of what happened, and tell us how you proved it."

By selecting the facts as they did and interpreting them within their own perspectives, these experts give very different points of view about the prosecutor's presentation. Note that different people do not need to select different facts to still express different viewpoints. By keeping this example in mind, you can see how the facts that your professor and texts talk about represent a certain point of view and do not speak for themselves.

Here is one more example of how the same fact can take on a whole different meaning depending on how it is stated:

> RAMONE: In spite of the demands of international competition, we as a nation still managed to lift 30 percent of low-income people above the poverty line.
>
> BRIDGET: Despite our wealth of resources, we lifted a mere 30 percent of our nation's low-income population above the poverty line.

Notice that although Ramone and Bridget use *the exact same fact* (30 percent lifted above poverty line), what this fact means is quite different according to the speaker's perspective.

It is important to remember that this chapter focuses on *multiple* perspectives rather than *two* perspectives. The possible number of perspectives that can influence our views on a topic is by no means limited to two.

➧ TIP 3 Recognize your personal lenses and avoid projecting.

As an active learner, you need to be aware of your own "lenses" to help combat personal biases or distortions. We tend to view the people and events in our world through our own personal lenses, which frequently distorts the messages we receive. Often we project onto them what we are thinking or feeling, rather than trying to understand their unique points of view. Always try to remember to wonder how your perspectives might be influencing your beliefs or perceptions, and then think about what you could learn from other relevant perspectives. *Remember:* You are not the center of the universe. The way you see the world is not necessarily the way the world is.

➧ TIP 4 Strive to be open-minded.

How often have you recently tried to seek out a conversation with someone on a topic because you knew she would disagree with you? We hope that your answer is "many times," but we doubt that will be the case because we usually don't try very hard to see or seek out opposing points of view. We (as well as many experts) usually seek out points of views and opinions from people who have similar perspectives to ours. Such a bias greatly limits our learning horizons. If you want to grow and develop as a learner, you must be willing to change your viewpoints when there is good evidence to do so. By actively putting yourself in others' shoes and making yourself open to their ideas, you not only gain a valuable learning opportunity, but you also become a more empathic human being. You are actively taking other people's interests into consideration, one of the marks of an ethical person.

TIP 5   Identify sources where multiple perspectives are expressed.

Your view of the world becomes much richer when you expose yourself to views reflecting diverse perspectives. Your choices open up. There are many locations where you are especially likely to encounter multiple perspectives. To get you started, we have listed a few of our favorites.

- Talk to your classmates, trying to discover the basis for their differing beliefs. Most people do not agree completely on much of anything. Just talking to someone else can often make you aware of different viewpoints.

- Be attentive to current issues and the debates surrounding them. Current issues (abortion, health care, tax increases, education funding and standards, etc.) tend to receive a lot of media coverage and are good sources for studying multiple perspectives.

- Read the letters to the editor section of newspapers and magazines and follow Internet conversations about controversial issues. These sources offer a natural forum for people debating significant issues. They frequently contain arguments for opposing viewpoints on a variety of issues.

- Look for books whose very purpose is to present alternative perspectives. These are generally collections of articles that examine an issue (or multiple issues) from a variety of viewpoints. See for instance, *Race and Gender in the American Economy* by Susan Feiner, *Hot Topics* by Daniel Starer, any volume in the Greenhaven Press Opposing Viewpoints series, or the collections in the Taking Sides series published by Dushkin and the monthly issues of *Congressional Digest.*

TIP 6   Study unassigned readings that express perspectives different from those in your texts.

When professors choose books and readings, they usually select from many possibilities. Thus, unless your teacher makes an active effort to emphasize multiple perspectives, your courses expose you to a restricted range of possible perspectives. Check the library for other texts and readings, or ask your professor for references to readings that represent a different perspective. Such active learning will help you overcome important biases in your college learning.

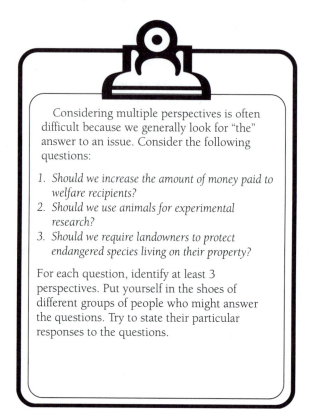

Considering multiple perspectives is often difficult because we generally look for "the" answer to an issue. Consider the following questions:

1. *Should we increase the amount of money paid to welfare recipients?*
2. *Should we use animals for experimental research?*
3. *Should we require landowners to protect endangered species living on their property?*

For each question, identify at least 3 perspectives. Put yourself in the shoes of different groups of people who might answer the questions. Try to state their particular responses to the questions.

QUICK REVIEW BOX

1. Understand that an expert has a perspective.

2. Be aware that facts don't speak for themselves.

3. Recognize your personal lenses and avoid projecting.

4. Strive to be open-minded.

5. Identify sources where multiple perspectives are expressed.

6. Study unassigned readings that express perspectives different from those in your texts.

PLACES TO SEARCH FOR MORE ON THIS TOPIC

Cynthia H. Guzzetti, ed., *Perspectives on Conceptual Change: Multiple Ways to Understand Knowing and Learning in a Complex World* (Mahwah, NJ: Erlbaum, 1998).

John Berger, *Ways of Seeing* (New York: Penguin Books, 1986).

Norman Melchert, *Who's to Say?: A Dialogue on Relativism* (Indianapolis, IN: Hackett Publishing Co., 1994).

http://www.libertynet.org/pa/kat/multiperspectives.html

EPILOGUE

LOOKING BACK AND MOVING FORWARD

We hope that your journey through this book has been much like the mountain climbing we talked about in the first chapter—challenging but doable, gradual but steadily moving forward, and very rewarding!

As you look back at the chapters you have studied, you will notice that obstacles to your learning can be conquered. While the tips for active learning are not all simple, you can find uses for each of them with frequent practice. We hope that you now see your teachers, texts, notes, friends, libraries, and other components of the college experience in somewhat of a different light after having read this book. They can all be useful to you as you work to understand a little more about yourself and our world.

Change is difficult and does not occur at once. Even when you have difficulties with particular tips, be excited that you are attacking those roadblocks to your learning excellence. The key to your ongoing improvement as an active learner is to keep striving to improve both your attitudes and strategies. *Remember:*

Strong Attitudes + Good Strategies = Excellence in College

As you look ahead to all that you will be learning, be proud of how far you have come. Sure you still have a long way to go; we all do. But each of the small steps you have taken toward excellence in college is a personal victory. Don't dwell on what you cannot yet do; instead, feel good about the tips that you have mastered and about your *trying* to master other tips. You have plenty of time to master more and more tips as you practice active learning.

You know all too well that being an active learner is a lot harder than approaching your life as if you were just a huge sponge. But we hope that you now appreciate how much more rewarding active learning can be. The *process of striving for excellence* can be exhilarating, giving new meaning to being in college. As professors, we would be flattered if we have somehow helped you become your own best teacher.